ADVANCE PRAISE FOR THE LOVE FIX

"This book is filled with hope, positivity, and all the tools you need to help your relationship thrive."

—John Gray, PhD, author of Men Are from Mars, Women Are from Venus

"An essential read for anyone in a relationship. No matter what the state of your relationship you will find tips and strategies in *The Love Fix* to enhance it, and to maximize your own happiness in the process."

—Louann Brizendine, MD, author of The Female Brain and The Male Brain

"Dr. Tara Fields has three decades as a couples therapist under her belt, but unlike most of her brethren, she also has had vast experience in the media. So she knows how to communicate. And you are the beneficiary. That's only one reason why this is the best relationship book I have ever read. It is wise and modern, but most importantly, refreshingly objective, down-to-earth, direct, and practical. This is a must-read."

—Dr. Dean Edell

"Tara Fields has combined the best of cutting-edge thinking in the fields of holistic psychology, mindfulness, and couples therapy to arm readers with the skills that will bring forth change and real transformation. A useful guide for clinicians as well as for couples and individuals who strive for healing change."

—Ronald Alexander, PhD, MFT

THE LOVE FIX

The
LOVE FIX

Repair and Restore
Your Relationship Right Now

TARA FIELDS, PhD, LMFT

WILLIAM MORROW

An Imprint of HarperCollins*Publishers*

HarperCollins books may be purchased for educational, business, or sales promotional use. For information please e-mail the Special Markets Department at SPsales@harpercollins.com.

FIRST EDITION

Infinity symbol icon © *by Alice Noir/Shutterstock, Inc.*
Endless love tattoo icon © *by Pavel Kryshtapovich/Shutterstock, Inc.*

Library of Congress Cataloging-in-Publication Data has been applied for.

ISBN 978-0-06-240721-4

15 16 17 18 19   OV/RRD   10 9 8 7 6 5 4 3 2

In loving memory of Jerry Fields,

who never failed to ask, "How's the book going?"

Dad, I think you would be proud.

♥

Contents

· · · · · · · · · · · · · ·

Introduction   1

1. How Did We Get Here?   17

2. How Can We Change?   33

3. The Parent Trap ∞ Equal Partnership   53

4. Come Close, Go Away ∞
   Interdependent Relationship   91

5. The Blame Game and the Shame Spiral ∞
   Ownership and Respect   129

How to Survive an Affair   172

6. Testing, Testing, 1, 2, 3 ∞ Profound Trust   175

7. Grow Apart ∞ Grow Together   203

8. The Owner's Manual   235

3 Things You Can Do Today for an Instant
Shift in Your Relationship   252

Afterword   255

Acknowledgments   259

Resources   263

Index   265

Introduction

I AM SO SICK of being ignored. You just never, *ever* listen." Sara clutched the tiny pillow to her chest and sank deeper into the sofa.

"I have no idea what you're talking about. I listen to you all the time."

"Really? Yesterday I told you that your mother called and announced she's coming to visit. And you just sat there. Did you even *hear* me?"

Sean looked perplexed. "I don't remember that."

"See? This is exactly what I'm talking about. You just sat there, watching the news. It's like you're more interested in the news than you are in me!"

"That's not true."

Sara crossed her arms tightly across her chest and glared at her husband. Her body language communicated frustration, and the disappointment beneath it. "Okay, then tell me the last time we sat down and really talked," she said, her voice rising in pitch. "When was the last time we did anything together, just the two of us? I can't even remember! Because you're always busy, or you're working, or you're watching the news while I'm trying to talk to you about something important."

"Oh God. Here we go again." Sean rolled his eyes, threw his hands in the air, and glanced at the clock reflexively, checking the time.

"See?" Sara pointed a finger in Sean's direction. "*This* is what he does. He just shuts down. I mean, it's so obvious that he doesn't care. He clearly doesn't care about me *or* this marriage."

With that, Sean fixed his gaze on the window of my Bay Area office and watched the rain fall softly on the redwoods, the heavy fog rolling in around the base of Mount Tamalpais.

As a licensed marriage and family therapist for more than twenty-eight years, I have counseled hundreds of clients, and almost all of them come to me because they're frustrated, heartbroken, stuck. Like Sara and Sean, they love each other, but something seems broken. They feel that they've changed or grown apart, or that too much has happened. They don't know how to fix their relationship, and they fear the only way forward is out.

Sound familiar?

If you've picked up this book, the great news is, you're here because you have the desire to make things better. No matter the problems you're facing and the baggage you've accumulated, you know that your relationship still has a chance; you remember the love and the passion you have shared, and you want a chance to find your way back to each other, back to the person you were and the person your partner was, and the couple you were together before everything started going wrong.

The problem is, it can seem like you don't even know where to start.

If you feel like you were absent the day they passed out love's rule book, you're not alone. None of us were given a rule book for how to communicate and create a loving relationship. So instead of playing by a common set of rules, we're pushed and pulled by the patterns we created in our childhoods and earlier relationships. With more than 50 percent of marriages ending in divorce, these aren't always the greatest examples. Too often we wind up feeling angry or misunderstood, and we react— hurting each other or retreating into hopelessness, and growing apart in the process.

By the time couples like Sara and Sean come to see me, they're usually so mired in conflict—individually feeling hurt and lonely—that they've resorted to assigning blame. I'm often asked, either directly or indirectly, to collude with one of them, to pick a side and confirm that the *other* spouse or partner is at fault. ("See? This is what he does. He just shuts down.") Each half of a couple can become so invested in trying to be "right" that knee-jerk reactions begin to take precedence over being loving and kind. They get to the point where to lose an argument seems like it means losing an essential piece of themselves, and they just can't let that happen. They lose all perspective and the ability to see that they're actively losing the chance of "winning."

And that's where I come in. Part of my job as a psychotherapist is to see couples with fresh eyes—and to remind them that no matter how bad things have gotten, they can get better. How do I know? Because there's a simple truth about all relationships that most of us miss: It's not the fighting or the resentment or the icy indifference or the fact that "he never listens." In other words, it's not *what* you're fighting about that matters. It's the *patterns* you fall into *when* you fight that can tear a relationship apart. Clients come in and say, "Tara, I don't get it. I have never loved anyone like this, and I have never had conflict like this. Am I with the wrong person? Should we just quit? Am I crazy? Did I make a mistake?"

No! If you're feeling this way, you're not crazy, and it doesn't mean you have made the wrong choice in a partner. Most often it means you made a good choice. There's a line I love from the book *A Course in Miracles,* published by the Foundation for Inner Peace: "Love brings up everything unlike itself . . . to be healed." Love brings up everything you have kept hidden away: unresolved wounds and traumas, fears. Perhaps you feel safe enough, vulnerable enough, in love to allow these old feelings and experiences to resurface. Letting love take the lid off Pandora's box frees those demons—and once they are free, they can be healed.

Here's what happens: you get a ring or move in together or you join hearts—you become part of someone else's world, and that person becomes part of yours—and then the conflict starts. Maybe it was there all along, and you thought this next step of commitment would make it all go away. Whatever the case, when the conflict starts or grows, you make the mistake of thinking it must be because you're with the wrong person. You say, "Hey, if I was with the *right* person, we wouldn't be fighting, right?"

But the important truth is that it's never all hearts and flowers. In fact, when you find the person you love and this person loves you back, that love will permeate the layers of protection you've built to keep yourself safe; it will get down to so many things you've never dealt with before. It may be exactly because you found the *right* person that you're fighting—now your heart is open; you're here in the moment, sitting with yourself in a way you never have before; and now you have the chance through this relationship to let these unresolved issues and fears bubble up from your past so that you can heal them in an authentic way. You have an opportunity: if you can reframe your relationship with conflict, not only can you find your way back to the passion and wide-eyed wonder you once felt in your relationship, but you can also use the safety of a relationship in which you reach out and your partner reaches back to learn more about *yourself.* Can you reframe this conflict as an opportunity not only to repair and strengthen the relationship with your beloved but also to heal your own wounds?

I have seen couples find peace, come closer together, save their relationships, and build relationships that last by simply understanding how they handle their problems and making some pretty straightforward changes to how they communicate. You would be surprised how many more relationships would work, how many more families would stay together, and how many more people would be happy and fulfilled in their relationships if they could take a step back from their conflicts. If you're fighting or locked in conflict right now, right as you read these words, you have one of the greatest opportunities of your life to connect deeply with your partner and with yourself. My hope is that this book—which explains and explores the five most common fighting patterns couples fall into, offers insight from couples who have broken out of those conflict loops, and provides the tools to help build a lasting relationship—will be a guide for you and give you the courage to reach for the beautiful relationship that is within your power to create.

 THE FIVE CONFLICT LOOPS AND THE FIVE CIRCLES OF LOVE

Circles have long been used to symbolize unity and inclusivity, the connectedness of all things. The roundness of the wedding ring, for example, represents an eternal bond between partners, an endless commitment. In Celtic culture, circles represent protective boundaries, warding off enemies and evil. We think of life as being lived in a circular pattern, from the repetition inherent in daily tasks to the larger cycle of birth and death.

When it comes to relationships, I like to think of couples coming together in a circle of love. Healthy relationships have a certain amount of back-and-forth, give-

and-take. You give your spouse or partner love, and your love is returned. You put energy into the relationship, and you gain energy in return.

However, circles symbolize more than inclusion and collaboration; they also symbolize futility. Think of a dog chasing its tail or those movie characters who get lost in the woods and always seem to return accidentally to where they started. Not only can you be contained and protected in a circle, but you can also be *stuck* in one. Recurring arguments can turn your circle of love into a conflict loop.

Take Sara and Sean. Sara was frustrated at never being heard. Sean was tired of being attacked. They seemed ready to throw in the towel—not because they didn't love each other, but because they had been spiraling downward for so long, they couldn't even imagine finding their way back to the loving relationship they had started with. He had a boatload of old wounds from his adolescence that he kept running away from. She tried to pull him close. He rejected her; and when his rejection pushed her buttons, she reacted with anger. When Sara and Sean came to see me, they were stuck in what I call the Come Close, Go Away conflict loop—a pattern that results from a slow progression of neglect and from turning a blind eye and being complacent.

But for each dark conflict loop, there is the light of a circle of love—a way that conflict is transformed into heart-forward understanding. The opposite of the Come Close, Go Away conflict loop is the Interdependent Relationship circle of love. How many couples do you know that are like Sara and Sean, or maybe like a version of Sara and Sean that isn't quite so extreme? How many couples do you think are stuck in simmering resentments that never quite break the surface? Couples can spend months or years or decades or even their whole lives in conflict without ever ripping off the Band-Aids to expose that conflict to the light of day. But if you can learn to recognize your conflict, you can transform it. It can seem like you're staring into the abyss of devastation, but right on this brink is also the opportunity to create the relationship you always imagined having.

In all, there are five conflict loops matched with five circles of love:

- The Parent Trap ∞ Equal Partnership
- Come Close, Go Away ∞ Interdependent Relationship
- The Blame Game and the Shame Spiral ∞ Ownership and Respect
- Testing, Testing, 1, 2, 3 ∞ Profound Trust
- Grow Apart ∞ Grow Together

Are you jumping up and down with your hand raised, like a kid in class, and saying, "That's me!" Sometimes it's obvious; all you needed was the name. Other times, these patterns can be harder to spot, especially if you're trying to spot a conflict loop from inside the relationship. In that case, you might need to keep reading through the stories, descriptions, quizzes, and exercises in this book before you find yourself. And there are a variety of reasons people fall into these patterns. You feel as if you must hide unlovable parts of yourself; your partner grows in directions you can't seem to understand or follow; there is a breach of trust that feels so wide, you will never see your way across to each other again. Some couples may even recognize more than one behavior pattern at work at a time. But regardless of which conflict loop you most identify with, once it starts, it reinforces itself, becoming harder and harder to break. Without some kind of intervention, this toxic cycle will only get worse.

Here's what else these loops have in common: conflict loops are created by a deep desire to be loved and understood. The person who endlessly attacks might be asking, "Do you love me enough? Am I important enough? How much can you take before you leave me, like everyone who came before you?" By understanding what your partner needs, even when they don't know themselves or don't know how to ask for it, and what you need yourself during these difficult and seemingly hopeless times, you can turn conflict into communication, understanding, acceptance, passion, and compassion.

I want you to think back over the course of your relationship. Was there a time when the two of you were passionately in love, when you treated each other as equals, when you were lovers as well as loyal friends? If you had that love once, if you had that passion, I promise you that you can get it back again. It takes work. To recognize the patterns at play, acknowledge them, and address them means exploring the fears, insecurities, old wounds, and unrealistic expectations that created them in the first place.

In relationships, there are two kinds of circles—one creates futility and frustration, while the other creates life, love, and a safe space. With the guidance in this book and hard work, you can change the conflict loops in your relationship into circles of love.

THE NUMBER ONE REASON RELATIONSHIPS FAIL

Contrary to popular opinion, snarky remarks, cold indifference, anger, and rude behavior generally don't come from a place of contempt. However counterproductive, these behaviors are "protections," ways to avoid more uncomfortable emotions, like fear or pain or shame. Most of us have good reason for occasionally shutting down or lashing out. For example, Sean withdrew from the conversation in my office as a way to avoid the pain and shame brought on by Sara's accusations.

Though they didn't realize it, Sean acted in a way that he believed kept him safe, and Sara acted in a way that she believed kept her safe. Maybe they learned these ways of acting during the course of this relationship, or maybe their ways of relating to each other developed long ago. Maybe as a child, Sean learned that waiting for time to pass while his parents were fighting or his mother was lecturing him—in other words, "checking out"—was the best way to protect himself from the distress caused by his parents' disharmony and from their judgment and emotional attacks. Now, as an adult behaving that way, he can seem petulant and dismissive, but when you look at *why* he's acting this way, you can dig back to a "good reason"—when he was a child, he learned to distance himself to protect himself from pain.

Now imagine what "good reasons" Sara could have for

needing reassurance. Maybe she grew up with a father who was unavailable and who eventually checked out altogether, while Sara's mother stuck her head in the sand. Maybe Sara had vowed to herself that this would never be her. Or perhaps she was complacent in her last relationship and regretted her decision not to work harder on it. Instead of sharing whatever fears she had with Sean, she just kept pulling. It was easy to see the makings of a conflict loop: these two individuals' behaviors lined up against each other in a way that created conflict. Sara had an emotional need that Sean wasn't meeting—and perhaps couldn't meet—and *he* had a need that *she* wasn't meeting. They were both acting in ways that triggered the other person's deepest fears. The question to explore—and you'll have many opportunities to do so in this book—is whether these behavior patterns (regardless of the reasoning behind them) are getting you what you want. Unfortunately, for Sean and Sara, and for so many couples I've seen over the years, their reactions to conflict, which were meant to keep them safe, ended up creating exactly the thing they were meant to guard against. Sean's distancing made Sara dig deeper for engagement; Sara's judgment made Sean pull away.

If you keep having the same argument over and over, consider it a sign that something similar may be going on in your relationship. Consider it a clue that *you're not really fighting about what you're fighting about* (something you'll hear me say throughout this book). Reactionary behaviors—the rude, nasty, or hurtful zingers that go straight to the heart; the accusations; the tendency to withdraw or retreat—may have worked as protections when you were a child or even when you were in previous relationships. But if you're reading this book, they ain't working now.

As an adult, you have choices. You don't have to be a slave to that fearful child who lives within you. Now you're ready to try something new. It's time to ask what you're really fighting about. What are you asking for that your partner is unwilling to give? And what is on the other side of this argument? What is your partner not getting that he or she needs to feel heard, understood, respected, loved, and fulfilled? Understand that *both* partners have a part in every conflict loop. Think about it: you can't sustain a Come Close, Go Away conflict loop unless one partner pushes and the other pulls.

In the heat of the moment, however, the last thing people want to do is take responsibility for their part in the conflict. No one wants to stop and say, "Gee, let me step back and take ownership for *my* part." It's difficult to accept responsibility and normal to avoid it. But it can become a major problem when couples become like dogs with a bone, rabidly insisting that their problems are—solely and completely—the other person's fault. "*He* doesn't listen." "*She*'s clingy and needy. It's all *her* fault." "It's all *his* problem." Looking at your part in the matter is a crucial part of the process.

TAKE A VACATION FROM THE LAND OF ME

It takes understanding your role *and* your partner's role in your relationship in order for the two of you to make the necessary changes that will help you find your way back to each other. If you want to save your relationship, you have to be willing to do the work. How you behave is linked to how your partner will behave, and changing how you direct your energy has the power to change the entire cycle.

Are you the one who picked up this book? Are you scared that your partner won't join you in revamping your relationship? Let go of your fear. The only way to move forward is to be brave enough to be vulnerable. This means temporarily putting aside your own needs and getting out of what I call the land of "it's all about me," the Land of Me, a place where everything points back to you. In the Land of Me, you live in your own *circle*, in which you hoard everything good and deflect everything challenging or "bad."

When in the Land of Me, one or both members of a couple are:

- Shouting
- Blaming
- Shaming
- Accusing
- Right/Wrong

- Walled off or shut down
- Inflexible
- Complacent
- Reactive
- Walking on eggshells

When not in the Land of Me, one or both members of a couple are:

- Choosing to pause
- Taking a breath to choose how to react
- Soft and open
- Curious
- Asking themselves what the loving response would be

- Letting go of the assumption that there is only one "right" way
- Taking ownership
- Looking at the opportunity the conflict presents

Do you see aspects of the Land of Me in the description of Sean and Sara? Do you see some of these aspects in your own relationship? As we make this journey together, please keep in mind that the stories I use as illustrations are drawn from real life but aren't about one individual or couple. I chose these stories because I have seen these same conflicts often and have heard these exact words from many, many different individuals and couples over the years. The scenarios are real, but the names and professions and other details have been changed.

As you read, you might think, *That's me!* or *That's us. That is exactly what my husband/wife/partner does!* When you see yourself in these stories, rather than feeling less unique, I hope you feel less alone. And when the transformation in your relationship doesn't happen as quickly as it does for the couples in these stories, know that you're not alone in that, either. I wish the process of healing a relationship were as easy as making a few insightful observations and suggesting a few behavioral changes. Alas, in real life, at real-life speed, identifying the conflict loops (and there is often more than one at work), beginning to shift the way you typically argue, sustaining change over a long period of time, and doing the work required to find or restore your circle of love takes time and patience, commitment and courage.

But I promise you that if you also have a strong commitment to change, you can rebuild, restore, and rekindle the passion and companionship you once had. If you can manage to take a vacation from the Land of Me, the entire dynamic of your relationship will begin to shift, little by little. So on to the first big question. . . .

ARE YOU IN OR ARE YOU OUT?

This is one of the first questions I ask couples that come in together for couples therapy: "Are you in or are you out?" Of course, this is a way to ensure that both partners are committed to what will be a rigorous process of discovery and change. But it also creates a visual goal. Are you willing to step into a circle of love, or are you committed to the conflict loop, which has become so habitual, so comfortable in its toxicity?

This is your first step, too. *Are you in or are you out?* For now, just *wanting* to be "in," even if you don't quite know how to do it yet, is enough. These conflict loops are not something you fall into overnight. It is hard enough to change how we handle conflict on our own. Add another person to the mix, and it is twice the work. Are you willing to commit to this work—the work that is needed to step *into* a circle of love?

The Love Fix will give you the tools you need to begin turning your relationship around—these are the same tools I have given to countless couples in my practice. You'll find a combination of exercises, including what I call "3-Minute Fixes"—tips you can start using right this second to begin breaking through those destructive patterns. In the HEARTwork exercises, you'll be asked to dig deeper, to start recognizing and grappling with the hurts, pains, and fears that lie beneath your actions.

I have seen some of the most loving, passionate, and fulfilling relationships blossom between couples who have used these tools, despite the fact that they had been getting it wrong for years. I have seen spouses bounce back from the brink of divorce to experience a love that is even stronger than what they had when they started. I am telling you, it can happen.

Miracles can happen, even if your partner won't join you in this process. Whether you're newly dating, at your silver anniversary, or single and hopeful, by learning to recognize, interpret, and empathize with your own and your partner's yearnings and desires during the rough patches, you can prevent and reverse problem patterns and build, rebuild, and maintain fulfilling bonds and relationships that last.

Chapter 1

• • • • • •

How Did We Get Here?

NOT SO LONG ago, I made plans to meet up with an old friend of mine for lunch. I arrived first at the restaurant and chose a table outside. It was a gorgeous day— sunny, cloudless skies, a cool breeze—and the patio was packed with people enjoying one of the Bay Area's legendary Indian summers. Seated at the table next to me was a couple in their late twenties, holding hands, wedding rings glinting in the sun.

I remember noticing how gentle they were with each other—staring attentively into each other's eyes, laughing together at some private joke. *Isn't that wonderful?* I thought, enjoying a few quiet moments to myself while waiting for my friend to arrive. Then I heard the sound of an iPhone alert—one of my table neighbors had an incoming text.

"Looks like the guys are switching the bike ride from Saturday to Sunday," the husband said, checking his phone with his free hand.

His wife immediately pulled away. "I hope you're not saying yes."

"Well, yeah . . . ," he said, busy tapping out a response. "It's the weekend bike ride!"

"Right, but Sunday is our family day. You know, the farmers' market? Dim sum?"

"Oh, relax. It's just this once."

I could see his wife growing more agitated by the minute. "But, honey, we had plans."

"It's *one time*," he said, exaggerating the words for emphasis. "I don't know why you always have to blow everything out of proportion."

The fight quickly snowballed, and it was heartbreaking. One minute they were holding hands, and the next they were getting swept up in a knock-down, drag-out fight about something as simple as weekend plans.

All couples argue, but how do some couples get *here*, to what seems like the point of no return? How do they go from experiencing the euphoria of that first kiss, the overwhelming feeling of happiness when they realize they've found "the one," the bliss of thinking ahead to their future together, to wondering what they ever saw in each other in the first place?

Here's the thing: in a relationship, you almost never fight about what you're fighting about. Whether you realize it or not, you're fighting about something that happened last night or a year ago, or you may even be rehashing issues from your previous relationships or reenacting struggles that existed in the family you grew up in. You may *think* you're arguing about a bike ride or dinner plans, or where to spend the holidays or how to spend your money, and you may think you're having lots of different arguments about lots of different things. But actually, it's much more likely that you're having the same fight again and again, a fight that comes in many different guises, reflecting what seems most irksome on any given day.

SAME FIGHT, DIFFERENT NIGHT

Most of the time when a couple comes into my office, I know it's only a matter of time: once everyone has had their say in a safe, controlled environment, what they're really fighting about—the fear beneath the anger—is going to emerge. That's why they can't "just get over it." That's why they keep fighting about the same thing over and over again. It's not really about dirty dishes in the sink or the choice of weekend plans. It's about questions such as: "Do you love me?" "Do you really hear me?" "Am I important to you?" "Are we ever going to have sex again?"

Not only do you and your partner bring your own unconscious ways of living or relating to the relationship, but when you come together, so does your raw material, creating new patterns of its own. The more you allow your reactive responses and your personal agenda to drive the relationship, the more they bounce against each other in ways that create conflict loops. And the longer these conflict loops last, the harder it is to break free of them.

Only by digging into and exploring the behavior can you get at what you were *really* fighting about, at the original conflict. Only by bringing that conflict out of the shadows and into the light, by pulling it up by the root, can you ensure that it doesn't keep coming back as a new fight in disguise. Was this couple at the table next to me fighting about a bike ride? Hardly. But if not a bike ride, what were they *really* fighting about? What are you really fighting about in your own relationship?

THE SIX MOST COMMON SOURCES OF RELATIONSHIP CONFLICT

In every conflict loop explored in the chapters that follow, discovering the deeper issue at play is the key to moving from the conflict loop into a circle of love. But there are also common sources of conflict in a relationship that aren't confined to any one loop. Identifying and understanding these sources of conflict will help you to become more aware of your actions, so it's worth getting a preview now.

You're Pushing My Buttons!

Were you the golden child or the black sheep of the family? Were you rewarded for your accomplishments or shamed for your failures? Were you encouraged to join the science club or prodded to play team tennis—just like your dad did—even though your heart wasn't in it? Or were you left to find your own path, with little guidance . . . and maybe even less support? The experiences you had when you were young shaped your personality, while the various relationships you forged—with your parents, siblings, friends, and romantic partners—created deep-seated fears, insecurities, wounds, and expectations. No one in the world is immune to their past. We all have issues. Maybe you've been dealing with your issues your whole life. Maybe you've never dealt with them. Maybe you didn't even know you *had* issues until now. Sometimes the act of falling in love is the catalyst for the emergence of the very barriers to love—it takes being in a circle of love to open up enough to let these issues leak to the surface.

Profound love can leave you feeling profoundly vulnerable. When you love deeply, you have more at risk. That feeling of unease or uncertainty (*What if he leaves me? What if, eventually, we split up?*) can tap into fears that lie at the very core of your being (*Am I lovable? Am I good enough?*).

In my work with individuals, couples, and families, I've found that unresolved trauma and pain from our past are the *primary* barriers to being able to maintain healthy relationships in the present. Rather than healing these wounds, however, we often project them onto our partner. You've heard (and probably used) the phrase "You're pushing my buttons," right? Well, your own "buttons," as well as your partner's, were installed long before the two of you even met. And by inadvertently pushing each other's buttons, you have the makings of a perpetual conflict loop.

What if the frustrated husband I observed at lunch, for example, felt as though respecting his weekend bike ride was a way his wife could show him appreciation for how hard he worked during the week? What if going to the farmers' market every Sunday would never be enough for her? What if, based on her history, she would always need extra affirmation that family came first? The couple from the restaurant likely wasn't having an argument about Sunday plans at all; they might have been locked in an escalating power struggle, one where the importance he placed on "me" time conflicted with her ideas about what it meant to be a "we." Whether you call it baggage, buttons, or issues, the only way to break a cycle like this is to explore where it comes from, to determine if disproportionately strong reactions to seemingly small events—like becoming irrationally, smoke-coming-out-of-your-ears angry when your partner wants to, say, change up the weekend plans—are *really* triggered by the present circumstance or by old fears that are exploding back into your life.

It could be a recurring fight or it may not even be a fight at all. In this book, you will learn to dig to the root of the issue, and in my experience it's often an insecurity or fear or question or mistaken belief about yourself or about love. The basis for this recurring conflict is the small child who sits at the heart of you or your partner—or, more likely, both of you—a child who is looking for empathy, who is desperately in need of love, but who doesn't know how to ask for it, accept it, or recognize it, even when it's right in front of him or her.

Great Expectations

Most serious relationships begin with, or at least work their way toward, high hopes. Even if an "I do" is not the goal, you and your partner at least have the intention to pursue a lifelong commitment. Unfortunately, this unspoken expectation can be one of the few that partners really agree on. In fact, one of the most common pitfalls I see among couples is when one or both partners enter a relationship with unrealistic, unexplored, or unspoken expectations.

Let's go back to the married couple at the restaurant. What if the wife, for example, believed that after they married, she and her husband would do absolutely everything together? They'd go grocery shopping, pick out bath mats and towels, and have double dates with all their friends rather than going their own way for boys' or girls' night out . . . or for a Sunday bike ride. What if she equated being married with never being alone or lonely? That constant companionship could be her expectation. And what if her husband's expectations were different? What if her husband saw marriage as a space in which he could finally go away to do his own thing, secure in the knowledge that the relationship would be there when he got back?

When we have different ideas about what a relationship should be, sometimes, without even meaning to, we end up disappointing each other in small, seemingly inconsequential ways. But over time those tiny disappointments add up. You would think that would be reason enough to discuss our expectations with each other. Yet most of us don't.

Why? I think it's because somewhere along the way, we

developed some really odd ideas about the power of love. We have these mythologies about finding "the one," these notions that our whole life's happiness hinges on finding the right person. *If I can find the perfect partner,* we tell ourselves, *I will have the perfect life.* We believe that years of emotional baggage will disappear without any work on our part. We believe that when we're *really* in love, it's supposed to be easy. We don't have to work on our relationship if we're perfect for each other, because everything just clicks . . . right? Love is enough!

Part of this naïveté is biological. In the earliest stages of attraction, our brains are flooded with feel-good chemicals. It's true what they say: love is as powerful and as addictive as any drug. But we often place so much emphasis on finding the "right" partner and then planning the wedding to end all weddings that we often forget to plan for—*hello!*—the rest of our life.

I'm not saying that you should lower your expectations about love. But there are things you can do to help a great love turn into happily ever after, and one of these things is discussing make-or-break issues, such as money, children, your in-laws, and religion, *before* making that major commitment. If you don't make a plan for how to handle things, big or small, together, as a team, you'll likely be blindsided when these issues inevitably come up. That's how you slip from a love with all the potential in the world to a state of consternation, in which you think, *Wait! We never talked about any of this! Are we going to have a joint checking account or individual accounts? Are we going to have kids now or later? Where are we going to spend the holidays?*

*What color bath mats do you prefer? Why is this so hard? I
thought love was supposed to be enough! And what about sex?*

Want to know why the divorce rate is so high? In part,
it's because we don't plan for the future, and then, when
the future hits and inevitable disagreements start, we still
can't look past the tips of our own noses. Any conflict *must*
be our partner's fault. We think, *I'm not as happy as I once
was, so I must be with the wrong person. If I'm not happy anymore, then this must not be Mr. or Ms. Right.*

This is why I feel so passionate about couples getting
some kind of premarital counseling, whether it's from a
marriage therapist, a minister or a rabbi, or even a weekend relationship intensive. And yet I have conversations
nearly every day—such as with the manager at my yoga
studio, the niece of a family friend, or the neighbor down
the street—in which people tell me, "Well, *our* love is different. Why spoil it by talking about money or the in-laws
or religion?" We don't talk about some of the most basic
issues—and we certainly don't talk about the more mun-
dane details of daily life—because it's not romantic, and
because (if we're willing to admit this) we're too afraid.

You may be afraid that sitting down with your partner to discuss these issues will create conflict. But by
not sitting down to discuss these issues, you can almost
guarantee conflict. And once your differing expectations
have been simmering for years, it can be much more of
a challenge to find compromise. (Also, if you have these
discussions late in the game and decide that you might be
better off with someone whose expectations match your
own, the consequences of that decision will be more dra-

matic than if you had talked early on.) You'll see this idea repeated in this book: often the things you do to avoid conflict create the exact conflict you're trying to avoid. You dodge the short-term pain but set yourself up for long-term pain.

If only we could dispel that fear and reframe these early discussions as an opportunity to bring up issues and resolve them before they turn into relationship-destroying time bombs. If you're willing to trust that discussing real-life issues won't "contaminate" the love you feel for one another, this process of discovery can actually safety proof your relationship. Knowing that you won't stumble onto one of these hidden time bombs in the future can make you more able to give your all to creating a circle of love in the here and now. A major difference between the fantasy of happily ever after and the reality of a circle of love that lasts is that the reality entails using your head, as well as your heart, to design the relationship with the intention of keeping misunderstandings that arise from different expectations from closing that connection between your open hearts.

Big Emotions

Big emotions can sometimes make us act stupid. When something our partner says or does hits a nerve in us—for instance, when it exposes an old, unresolved wound; fails to meet some expectation; or flat-out disappoints—we react. We get so swept up in our emotions that we forget what it means to be a loving, caring partner; all we can think about is hitting back, or proving that our partner is wrong and we are right—just like Sara from the Introduction ("You just never, *ever* listen") or the couple in the restaurant ("You always have to blow everything out of proportion"). Our knee-jerk reactions aren't just emotional; they're also physical.

The next time your emotions are triggered in this way, notice what happens in your body: your heart rate increases, your muscles tighten and clench, and you may even hold your breath. That's your body's sympathetic nervous system kicking in; more commonly, we call this our fight-or-flight response. Fight or flight is a highly efficient and effective way of coping when we're confronted with actual physical danger. It is not so effective, however, when it is triggered by stress or anxiety—like the kind caused by long-term relationship woes—from which there is no immediate relief.

Want to know the long-term effects of ongoing relationship stress? It's no secret that stress and anxiety can make you sick. However, research from the Gottman Institute shows that over time, a stressful relationship can cause illness in women, but that the same isn't true for men. Men's bodies release the stress hormone cortisol when engaged in a conflict, and then it's gone; but when women release cortisol, their bodies tend to hold on to it much longer. The stereotype is that after a fight, a man can roll over and go to sleep, while the woman stays up all night, fuming. There may be some truth in this, since in most (but not all) couples, the man gets rid of stress hormones more quickly than the woman does. Unfortunately, over the long term, high-stress relationships may weaken a woman's immune system, putting her at higher risk for everything from the flu to cancer.

Focusing on the Negative

Over time, the very things about your partner that you once thought were charming can start to drive you a little nuts. The man you once cherished for his sense of adventure and spontaneity can begin to seem childish and irresponsible. A partner you once respected for her maturity and work ethic now seems dull.

In the beginning, it's usually small stuff that elicits an occasional negative response—the socks he keeps leaving strewn across the floor, the fact that she always shows up late for dinner. Over time, however, this tendency to notice the negative turns into a bad habit. Have you heard the saying "Neurons that fire together wire together?" Dwell on the negative long enough, and you can actually alter the neural pathways of your brain, until you become hardwired for the negative. You begin to take all the good things in your relationship for granted—you notice only the things your spouse or partner does wrong, and none of the things he or she does right. And you start forgetting all the stuff that made you think you'd found the man or woman of your dreams.

In the meantime, you tend to overlook the ways in which the things you focus on directly affect your partner's behavior. For example, if you spend all afternoon stressing about your fear that your partner will breeze right past you without so much as a hello when he gets home from work . . . he probably will. Why? Because when you feel uptight and anxious about something, it shows. Your body tenses up; you're likely sending signals that are destined to trigger the exact response you don't want. So, while you're worried about his behavior, he's probably thinking, *Oh God, there's that look again. She's getting ready to nag me.* That's when he retreats to the television or the quiet hum of his computer, without even bothering to greet you first. Your heart may sink, but your brain says, "Hey, I was right."

Life Happens

Maybe you thought that stable, high-paying job would last forever and that you'd soon have enough income to start saving for retirement and buy your dream home, and the financial stability to begin making that five-year plan come true. Then along came layoffs, and—*wham!*—your whole division went kaput. Maybe three years into a relationship, your beloved wife got a breast cancer diagnosis. Or the child you worked so hard to conceive turned out to be a handful. It's impossible to predict everything that life will throw at us, but one thing is certain: Life will not always go according to plan. Things happen, through no fault of our own, that we aren't prepared to handle. It doesn't even take a huge unexpected life event to create change—sometimes time itself is enough to make you or your partner start losing hope that you will achieve the life you envisioned. When change happens—when something forces you to adjust your expectations (remember those?), when life moves in ways that make you wonder who you are—the question is whether you and your partner will grow together or grow apart.

Change is a major fork in the road for many couples. At that point of change, will they both take the same path or choose to go their own ways, even while keeping the relationship? This "growing apart" is a common reason why couples split apart after many years together. Their relationship isn't static; it's not what it was yesterday and not what it will be tomorrow. If one partner endeavors to keep the relationship the same as it has always been, while the other grows, or if the partners respond in different ways to life events that force change, they can find themselves staring back at the circle of love they once shared, wondering why they now find themselves so far apart.

The "When, Then" Game

Working on a relationship is . . . Well, it's work. In fact, it's much easier to postpone working on our relationship until the "right" time, or until we think that we're "ready." The problem is, by the time we're ready or willing to change, it may already be too late, or, at the very least, some water might have accumulated under the bridge, making it much harder to go back and fix what's been wrong for so long.

It's not just the psychological difficulty of it all that can make you put off "fixing" your relationship. For example, have you and your partner ever agreed that when you have more money, you'll go on vacation or travel the world or go on a date night? Or have you reassured each other that once the kids go off to college or you get through the holidays, you'll have more room in your lives for quality time? Have you ever promised yourself that when you lose weight, you will feel sexy again or be happy? I call this the "When, Then" game—when X happens, then you will put the effort into your relationship. It's a dangerous game, one made more dangerous by the fact that we often don't realize we're playing it.

Sometimes, postponing something pleasurable may seem like the responsible, obvious choice (you're probably not going to plan a second honeymoon, for example, if your spouse or partner has just lost his or her job). Too often, however, we become so focused on putting things off until tomorrow that we postpone our happiness and miss out on opportunities to experience what's right in front of us, to celebrate our love and our commitment to each other today. Play the "When, Then" game long enough, and you may find yourself looking around and wondering, *What happened? Why have we been so unhappy for so long, and where did our happy life go?* You started with a circle of love, and then every time you said, "When X happens, we'll do Y for our relationship," it took you one step further from that circle and closer to a conflict loop. No single step pushed you over the edge. But over time these steps added up to miles. Now you need to travel these same miles to get back to the love you once had.

Every playwright knows that conflict is an essential piece of every story. Conflict is also an inevitable and normal part of any relationship. It does not mean your relationship is better or worse than anyone else's, even those that (supposedly) don't have any conflict. Conflict isn't good or bad; what is important for strengthening your circle of love is how you handle the conflict. It's when these conflicts aren't resolved, and instead are left to fester, that they can grow into loops that keep you stuck. Now it's time to take a look at what you can do about them.

Chapter 2

• • • • • • •

How Can We Change?

A s i sat on the patio of the restaurant that day, listen-ing to a husband and wife argue about weekend plans, it occurred to me that both of them—despite the heated argument—might have actually been doing a whole lot of things right.

Perhaps the husband had been going along with fam-ily day at the farmers' market all this time because he recognized how important it was to his wife. Perhaps she wanted him to skip his bike ride simply because she believed in the power of family traditions. When you're present in the moment, conflict with your partner can become an opportunity to work through unresolved issues and to learn more about each other; it can even be a way to grow closer. Most of us, however, are pain-fully unaware of what's really going on when an argument breaks out. That's what was so painful for me, as a marriage therapist, when I overheard their exchange. Neither husband nor wife seemed able to stop and say, "Wait a minute. This is getting out of hand." If I could have waved a magic wand, their conversation would have gone something like this:

> **Him:** You know, we go to the farmers' market every weekend. I'm just curious. What's the big deal about changing up the plans this one Sunday? Why is this so important to you?
>
> **Her:** Well, I love our little rituals. I never had that growing up. We never spent time, you know, talking around the dinner table. I love that we have made spending time together as a family such a priority. I guess I thought it meant a lot to you, too. Does it not?
>
> **Him:** It means a lot to me because it means a lot to you. I love making you happy. But my weekend bike ride is something that makes me happy. When you make me feel bad for wanting to go, I don't feel appreciated for all the things that I do.

This version of the conversation includes the sort of nonjudgmental honesty and openness that creates genuine understanding. Since that day at the restaurant, I've thought of this couple often. Were they ever able to have that kind of productive discussion, or was this a fight that continued to build and build, until they were locked in a perpetual conflict about "me" time versus "we" time? I never found out, of course, because the next thing I knew, my friend arrived and I got swept up in my own conversation. But I have always wondered, would that couple ever realize all the wonderful things they were likely doing on one another's behalf? There was likely so much good there, if only they could see it.

I wish that I had been able to work with this couple. Sometimes it takes the guidance of a perspective outside the relationship for couples to become aware of their conflict loops. Change comes with awareness. If you can begin approaching your spouse or partner with curiosity—with a genuine desire to better understand what makes him or her tick—you can begin to identify (and help heal) the vulnerability that lies beneath his or her anger. If you can better understand why you're fighting, you can learn to transform a conflict with your partner into an opportunity to love each other more completely. Change comes with awareness. If you can learn how to see the pattern you've fallen into, you can teach yourself how to break it.

FOUR WAYS TO DIFFUSE CONFLICT

In the previous chapter we examined some of the common ways conflict is created in relationships. (We'll revisit these conflicts when looking at behavioral patterns later in this book.) Fortunately, there are also common ways to diffuse conflict—things that can be helpful no matter what type of conflict you are encountering with your partner.

I had been working with Audrey for five years when she showed up for her regular Tuesday appointment, happier than I'd seen her in ages.

"I think the work has really paid off," she said, plopping down on the couch. "I have to tell you what happened."

Audrey and her husband, Aiden, had been married for ten years. Recently, she explained, Aiden had been called away to New York on business, and he was due back in California at the end of the week. In the meantime, Audrey, an aspiring novelist, had received an invitation to attend a prestigious writers' workshop hosted by an award-winning author. She was elated and had immediately signed herself up. There was just one problem: Audrey would have to travel to L.A. on the same day that Aiden was scheduled to arrive home from the East Coast. When she had broken the news during their nightly phone call, Aiden had instantly become upset.

"He kept saying that he couldn't believe that I just signed myself up without even telling him," she said. "And that he didn't want me to go."

"What did you say?" I asked.

"Well, I was able to reframe this long before it even got close to escalating," she said. "I chose to step back before I reacted, to take a moment and think."

The "old Audrey," she explained, would have reacted. She would have immediately interpreted Aiden's response as an attempt to control her, and she would have pushed back. She likely would have accused Aiden of being selfish, and the conversation probably would have spiraled into an ugly fight and ended with a slam of the phone.

"This time, though, I was able to make the choice to see his reaction from a more curious, loving place. And I realized that he wasn't trying to control me. He loves me, and he wants to spend time with me. He was disappointed that I wouldn't be there when he got home. I realized just how grateful I am to have a husband who—after ten years of marriage—still wants to be with me. So many of my girlfriends are married to men who ignore them or tune them out. But my husband is saying, 'I miss you. I want more of you.' So many women I know would kill to have a husband like that!"

There is a precious moment that exists before any argument begins, a tiny window of opportunity that opens immediately after your partner finishes speaking and before you react or respond. Blink and you'll miss it. Our learned patterns of behavior can become so deeply ingrained that a nasty remark may escape our mouth before our partner has even finished speaking. That's why what Audrey managed to do—in the heat of the moment, no less—was so major. She chose to see the conflict not as a power struggle, but as a chance to better understand things from Aiden's point of view. When you make the conscious choice to give your partner the benefit of the doubt—by looking at things from a place of curiosity rather than from a place of judgment—the thing you're fighting about tends to fade away, leaving space for the loving behavior to follow.

Learning to find that little window that opens after your partner finishes speaking and before you react or respond isn't easy. It takes practice. To learn more about how to do it successfully, let's take another look at Sara and Sean as they continued arguing in my office.

"This is what I'm talking about," Sara continued. "He just doesn't listen. And that makes me feel like he doesn't care. Whenever I try to tell him how I'm feeling—"

"Here it comes," Sean interrupted. "Complaining, complaining, complaining."

"See? This is what he does! He just—"

"Okay, time-out," I said gently. "I feel like no one is breathing. So, we're all going to stop talking and just . . . take a breath."

Sean put his hands in his lap and inhaled, but Sara's eyes darted nervously around the room. After just a moment or two, she started in again. "What I was saying is—"

"No," I said, cutting her off. "Let's really take a breath. I don't think anybody is really in his or her own body right now. So, I want everyone to breathe . . . and exhale. Let's just come back to the moment and what is going on right now."

I stopped Sara and Sean because their conversation wasn't going anywhere. They were stuck in a reactive cycle: Sara was upset because Sean kept shutting down; Sean kept shutting down because Sara was so upset. (That's why we call it a conflict loop, right?) There's no use feeling bad about this, by the way. We've all been there. We have all had our buttons pushed and have started shouting, saying awful things that we don't really mean. When they react like this, some people report feeling helpless. In fact, I hear that all the time: "I can't help myself. I just get so angry, I react. I don't know how to stop!"

But remember, change comes with awareness. The first step to breaking the cycle of reactivity is to recognize when your emotions are being triggered, to be conscious of the fact that you're about to react (instead of waiting until after you have reacted to look in the rearview mirror of your life with horror). Is your heart pounding? Are your fists clenched? Are you grinding your teeth? Are you breathing heavy or holding your breath? These are all signs that your sympathetic nervous system is kicking in. And there's your window—that tiny glimmer of opportunity to actively choose what you're going to do or say next.

Notice, too, that I asked Sara and Sean to take a breath. Conscious, focused breathing requires paying careful attention to the air rising in and out of your lungs, and temporarily shutting out all other thoughts and distractions. It triggers the body's parasympathetic nervous system, the natural, biological answer to our fight-or-flight response. Deep breathing releases a flood of hormones that slow the heart rate, unclench muscles, and lower blood pressure. In other words, giving yourself a time-out—taking just thirty seconds to realize that your emotions are being triggered and then to breathe—is often enough to calm the situation down. It won't magically cure the anger, but it may prevent you from reacting in your habitual negative way.

Once you've recognized that your buttons have been pushed and you've stopped to take a breath, you can ask yourself, "What is my intention? Do I need to win this argument? Do I need to be right? Or do I want to be a loving and supportive partner? Am I taking ownership of my actions and words, or am I reacting? Am I helping the situation right now or making it worse?" The opposite of reactivity is intention. Taking thirty seconds to consider your actions and responses and how they do or do not match your intention can help you stay focused on creating a loving circle, rather than being led blindly by your bad habits into a conflict loop.

We all have an abundance of opportunities to practice breathing through our reactivity in our daily lives—on the highway, in the grocery store, at work, and with our kids, for sure! No pressure, my friend. Just set the intention to try. Don't expect perfection. It's like building a muscle: eventually, with practice, you will start to replace the automatic negative response with a more thoughtful, positive one.

Coming Back to Your Body

Our changing culture has required us all to become highly skilled and efficient multitaskers: We eat meals in front of the television while checking sports scores or status updates on our mobile devices. We field phone calls while driving to work while planning what we're going to make for tonight's dinner. Although we're often doing multiple things at once, rarely are we focused on any one of them. This is a mindless way of living. The antidote to a life that demands a kind of mindless, reactionary way of existing is mindfulness meditation, the purpose of which is learning to focus on one single thing at a time and being completely present and aware of what is going on in any given moment.

I've been incorporating the practice of mindfulness into my personal life, as well as my work with my practice, for decades. I'm pleased to see that it's gaining such widespread popularity, because it's an effective and powerful tool for managing reactivity and for getting in touch with our actual feelings. We're not so easily affected by outside triggers when we're truly present in the moment. Being mindful can help us self-regulate, as well as manage our personal relationships in positive, more productive ways.

For example, one of my clients, Monica, experiences an intense wave of anxiety whenever her husband, Ted, a stay-at-home dad, complains about the fact that she often works late. She feels an immediate urge to pull back or shut down. Not surprisingly, this seems only to make her husband more insistent and Monica more anxious, and it ultimately creates more distance between them. (This is another example of a conflict loop in which his need butts heads with her need in a way that feeds the conflict.) In one of our earliest sessions together, Monica and I spoke a bit about how mindfulness can help in a situation where you're about to react. So, a few weeks later, when Ted made a snarky comment about Monica having missed their son's soccer match to take a conference call, she thought to herself, *Okay, I realize something is being triggered in me. But now what? I need to know the next step.*

When your body is about to take over, it's helpful to bring yourself back to the present moment. Thus, back in the office, after Monica recounted the incident, I asked her to close her eyes, place her hands on the tops of her thighs, and take a few slow, deep breaths. "Now, where in your body do you feel tense?" I asked.

She thought about that for a moment. "Well . . . I guess in my stomach."

"Okay, and what do you feel in your stomach?"

"It feels . . . fluttery? Like I have butterflies, almost like I can't breathe. I feel it in my chest a little, too. I feel anxious," she said.

For the first time in a long time, Monica was being present and connecting with her feelings, rather than running from them. Learning to recognize when her anxiety was starting to take over her body by employing mindfulness could lead to change for Monica.

Cultivating Gratitude

In a relationship, everything our partner says and does affects us directly, and everything we say or do affects our partner. You get back what you put in. If the relationship is a circle of love, you contribute love and your partner returns it to you magnified. If the relationship is stuck in a conflict loop, negativity breeds only negativity.

What happens when your partner pays you a sincere and heartfelt compliment or goes out of his or her way to do something thoughtful for you? It doesn't just make you feel good—it makes you all the more likely to return the favor. According to research published in *Social Psychology Quarterly*, choosing to focus on and acknowledge the positives in your relationship creates new neural pathways, fundamentally altering the internal structure of your brain. With enough practice, you can override that overwhelming negativity; instead of noticing what your spouse or partner does wrong, you can begin to see all the things he or she is doing right.

True, this may be easier said than done if you've been stuck in a years-long downward spiral. Sometimes, couples come to my office with so much animosity that when I ask them to list some things they love about each other, they look at me like I'm nuts. And yet, little by little, those positive feelings and memories start to come back. One partner might admit that the other is actually a pretty great parent. Another might thank his or her partner for being an excellent and stable provider. That's how you begin creating a new, healthy pattern—by working at it.

When couples come in and it's clear they are focused on blaming and can't remember what they like, much less love, about each other, I start the session by having them each share five things they like about their partner or they're thankful for. I really do hold their feet to the fire, and they look at me like I'm out of my mind. The things they share don't have to be big—one client mentioned that his longtime girlfriend knew that he liked popcorn cooked in coconut oil, not butter or olive oil. Even things that may seem silly or trivial to you have meaning for your partner, as they make him or her feel loved and secure in the knowledge that you "get" him or her like no one else.

As difficult or as strange as it may feel at first to look

at your relationship from a new perspective—especially if you're used to just being angry—it's worth the effort. It's amazing how you can really start finding those things you love about a person. Once a couple makes this commitment, the walls start coming down, the tension in the room drains, and the partners start to soften toward each other. It may not be easy at first, but it's an important exercise, one that I recommend couples do daily. This book includes many tools like this. For instance, later we'll look at how to infuse gratitude into your relationship.

3 SECRET INGREDIENTS FOR A LASTING RELATIONSHIP

In my practice, not only have I discovered the five conflict loops and the circles of love they can become, but I've also seen what couples need to do to get from one to the other. Being mindful is a step in the right direction. But it also takes three very special ingredients. Let's look at how the practices in this chapter can work together to create the 3 Secret Ingredients for a Lasting Relationship.

The first secret ingredient is *intention*. Why are you reading this book? I'm guessing it's to rescue—or at least to improve—your relationship, to reconnect with or feel closer to your spouse or partner, to have more love in your life. And yet it's so easy to act contrary to this intention. You want to be right; you want to win; you want to do whatever it takes to stop the pain immediately. Unless you can consciously manage your intention, these wants can get in the way of what you really want: a circle of love. Let's go back to Sara and Sean, the couple in my office who had at least restrained their reactivity long enough to take a breath.

"Okay, let's try this again," I said. "Which one of you is going to let go of the need to be right? Who's going to try to see things from their spouse's point of view?"

"Honestly," Sara said, "I feel like we've been fighting about who's right and who's wrong forever. It's always been this way."

"Always?" I asked. "It's *always* been this way? If that's actually true, then I'm wondering, why did you ever get married?"

They both chuckled.

"Well, okay. It hasn't always been this way," Sara conceded. "I remember how it used to be . . . when we were dating, even when we first got married. I couldn't wait until the end of the day to see him! At the time, he was working really hard, but we still managed to find time for date nights. I really liked that."

"Sean, can you tell Sara something that you appreciate about her?" I said.

"Well, Sara is a terrific mother," Sean said. "Really, she is amazing with the kids. I don't know what they would do without her."

"That's nice to hear," Sara said, sitting up a little in her seat. "Sean works really hard to make sure that the family is taken care of. I've always known that I could count on him for that."

Now Sean perked up a little. "Okay, my turn. I love that she makes an effort to have a relationship with my mother, even though I know she can be . . . difficult."

"I can't tell you how wonderful it is to hear you say that. I have been trying really hard with your mother." Sara dabbed at the corners of her eyes with a tissue. She even laughed a little bit.

As Sara spoke, I noticed how present and focused Sean was. "Take a look at your husband," I said.

She nodded. "This is the first time in a long time that I feel like he's really listening to me."

Clearly, there had been and still was love between Sean and Sara, only it had been buried for so long by this conflict loop. We had reached the second of the 3 Secret Ingredients for a Lasting Relationship: a willingness to exercise *emotional courage*. When we talk about courage, there are really two kinds. Physical courage refers to being tough, being brave; while emotional courage is the ability to manage scary feelings and take emotional risks. This book is about exercising your emotional courage.

Often one partner will be a rock star when it comes to a capacity for emotional courage, accessing, facing, and expressing his or her feelings easily. Maybe the other partner has physical courage. For some, talking about feelings and engaging with others is fun, a recreational sport. For others, talking about or confronting feelings is about as much fun as a trip to the dentist.

My husband, Eric, is a fearless mountain biker. The sport lets him go to his happy place. When we met, his passion for mountain biking was obvious, and I wanted to support and share this passion . . . so I took up the sport myself. Thanks to Eric's patience and cheerleading, and the trust I have in him that he will never put me in harm's way, I have learned to see slopes that at first turned me into a scared bunny as fun and enlivening. Now if you hear or see a middle-aged woman barreling down Mount Tamalpais, screaming "Weeeeee!" that's me!

On the other hand, when Eric and I were first dating, he had trouble finding the words to express his feelings (not unusual for many men and for some women). If I were to fast-forward more years than I'll name, I would find myself finishing the rewrites for this book, while at the same time my beloved father was in hospice care at his home in Los Angeles. My husband was in L.A. and by my dad's side a full day before I arrived from San Francisco. When I arrived, the hospice nurse, who had been at the side of dying loved ones and their families for decades, shared with me that in all her years of doing what she did, she had never witnessed a son-in-law express the kind of love, kindness, and heartfelt appreciation that Eric had been able to express at my father's bedside.

Eric shared with me later that a decade ago he wouldn't have been able to access these feelings or forge the connection he had had with my dad while he was dying. He experienced an authentic and meaningful awareness about how much he had grown since we met, which touched him deeply. And, of course, this touched my heart and deepened my love and gratitude for my husband. The beauty of being in a relationship is that if a particular ability comes naturally to your partner but does not to you, or vice versa, you can use your partner's strength in this area to develop more of this ability in yourself. You should appreciate your partner's skill in nurturing what is lacking in you. That's the beauty of being a team. That's the beauty of being partners.

Reactionary behaviors—snarky remarks or accusations, a tendency to withdraw or retreat—allow us to avoid the real issue; they cover up, and distract us from, more painful and vulnerable emotions that we aren't ready or are too afraid to reveal. Sara, for example, was afraid that Sean didn't love her anymore, that he no longer cared about her or their marriage, so she got angry and lashed out ("You just never, *ever* listen"). Sean felt overwhelmed by Sara's anger, so he withdrew, perpetuating the very power struggle she was trying to avoid. One of them had to be the bigger or more courageous partner in order to let go of their agenda and be vulnerable. Sara might risk the pain of further rejection by sharing her fears. Sean, instead of shutting down, might share how he feels when he perceives that Sara is pulling on him. There are no guarantees of how the other person will react, no safety net. Just a strong individual commitment to change.

Change comes with awareness. Be kind, and lighten up on yourself and your partner. At one point in time these choices and behaviors (shutting down, fighting to be heard, needing to be right) were actually brilliant ones and might have been the only ones you had as a child (if your parents were raging, if a parent emotionally or physically abandoned you, if you were in a situation where you felt as though you had no control). These behaviors worked to protect you.

The questions to ask yourself at this point in your life are: "Are these behaviors *really* protecting me from what I fear? From rejection, loneliness, or my uncertainty that I am being loved for my authentic self?" If you dig deep, I think you'll find that the answer to both questions is no. So read on! You are about to embark on a wonderful, growth-promoting, love-inducing journey.

In order to begin to unravel toxic relationship patterns, you need to muster the emotional courage to put your anger aside and confront the uncomfortable fears that provoked it. You need to be motivated and willing to be open and honest enough to discover if those fears you've been harboring—"Does he still love me?" "Will I ever be able to get it right?" "Will she ever stop being angry?" or "Is this marriage over?"—are actually true.

Emotional courage also includes making yourself vulnerable to your partner when you're not sure your partner will accept your olive branch. What if you reach out and find your partner is no longer there? What if you are the first to step into that space that is halfway between the two of you and your partner doesn't step into it to meet you? Even admitting there is a middle ground between your position and your partner's position takes courage. Ask yourself what you are most afraid of. If you're reading this book, you are probably most afraid of losing your relationship. And here's the thing: If you don't find the emotional courage to do the scary thing, to lay yourself open to your partner, the relationship is almost certainly doomed. If you can find the courage, you've got more than a fighting chance. So why not take that first step?

"I don't want to nag you to death," Sara said to Sean. "I don't want to be fighting all the time. I just get scared, especially when I feel like you're not really listening.

I worry that maybe you don't want to do this anymore."

"No, I do. I love you, and I want to be there for you. I want to hear you more, but sometimes I just don't know how to give you what you want. I get frustrated with all the fighting, so I want to go away and be by myself."

And that brings us to the last of the 3 Secret Ingredients for a Lasting Relationship: *hope*. Couples come to my office because they have hope. You're reading this book because you have *hope*, too. There's a reason you're here with me, with these couples, and with yourself in these pages. That reason is that no matter how bad it's gotten, no matter how long you've been spinning around in a devastating conflict loop, no matter how much time has passed since you were in that circle of love that you used to have, you haven't given up hope.

SET YOUR INTENTION AND GO FORWARD WITH HOPE

It can be easy to forget all the ways in which our actions trigger reactions in our partner. Before you know it, a simple misunderstanding can descend into yet another run-through of your conflict loop, which doesn't lead to a resolution, but only to resentment and increasing unhappiness. Recognizing when your emotions may be out of proportion to the situation, stopping to take a breath, and reminding yourself of your intention can help you and your partner get back on track. Next I've provided what I call a "3-Minute Fix," an exercise designed to help you master a particular skill. Throughout the following chapters, you will find 3-Minute Fixes designed to help you through the challenges you are experiencing; and at the end of each of the next five chapters, you'll find a quiz and a series of HEARTwork exercises designed to help you break out of the specific conflict loop to which that chapter is devoted.

This chapter's 3-Minute Fix is geared toward honing your mindfulness, which is a powerful tool for managing reactivity and getting in touch with your intention. Don't be deceived by the name "3-Minute Fix." Three minutes is all you need to adjust your point of view and see your relationship through a new lens that promotes real change.

3-MINUTE FIX ♥

PRACTICING MINDFULNESS

Ideally, you'll make an effort to use mindfulness regularly as a tool as you work toward restoring your circle of love. Here's a great way to start: Using the statements and questions that follow as a guide, take a few moments to think about your personal intention right now. Keep it simple and choose just one intention for now. The surest way to succeed is to set small attainable goals.

- I want to stop snapping at my partner.
- I want a more peaceful home for our children.
- I want to look at my part in our conflict.
- I want to be open and available to my partner.
- I want to have an open and honest relationship.
- I desire to be more affectionate and/or to receive more affection.

- I want to replace hostility and conflict with peace in my relationship.
- I want to replace old grievances with forgiveness.
- I would like a renewed sense of connection and more quality time together with my partner.
- I want to build or rebuild trust.
- I want more personal space, or "me" time.
- I want more passion and sex.
- I want to play more with my partner and have fun together.

Take as much time as you need, and have a really honest moment with yourself. Then record your intention below and keep it at the front of your mind as you continue reading.

My intention is to _____

_____

Chapter 3

• • • • • • •

The Parent Trap ∞
Equal Partnership

THE PARENT TRAP conflict loop usually starts with good intentions, from a place of genuine love and caring. The person who falls into it may be a wife who is determined to help her husband eat healthy and give up his fast-food habit, but then she ends up checking the corners of his mouth for ketchup when he comes home after work and looking for wrappers under his car seat. Or this person may be a husband who knows his wife hates doing the paperwork related to bills and mortgages, and so he offers to take this chore off her plate . . . but then ends up holding the purse strings. Think about the imbalance of responsibility for certain things in your relationship. Is it about being helpful or about being in control? Together, when you support each other's weaknesses, you can make a team that's stronger than the two of you individually. But when support becomes control, that's the start of the Parent Trap.

This chapter is about rebalancing power and responsibility in a way that allows each partner to see his or her beloved in a new light and show respect for his or her contribution to the relationship. It's about moving from a conflict loop—in which one partner acts like the parent by checking up on the other's performance or (mis)behaviors, while the other throws responsibility out the window—to an equal partnership between adults and lovers.

Again, unlike some of the other conflict loops in this book, the Parent Trap often has its roots in healthy and loving behavior that comes from the heart. You might have started taking on responsibilities that come naturally to you in an effort to make things easier and to care for your partner, yet slowly this turned into unhealthy and controlling behavior. For example, what starts out as you keeping the family calendar can slip into a situation in which you are responsible for making sure your partner is where he or she needs to be at every moment of every day. Then again, some relationships may work just fine when tasks are split: he is in charge of the calendar, she is in charge of paying bills, he is responsible for cooking a healthy dinner, and she is responsible for making vacation plans. It's about finding what works for you. And let's face it—as much as you kvetch (complain) about the calendar or vacation plans, if it isn't your thing, then you know deep down that it can be pretty nice to have your partner taking care of it for you.

The Parent Trap happens when overall responsibility or power or the perception of competence gets out of balance, such as when one partner decides that the other could never be in charge of the family calendar, because he or she would mess it up. Or when one partner decides that after what happened last time, the other partner will never be allowed to make vacation reservations ever again— otherwise they'll end up in a dingy cabin with an outside shower.

The Parent Trap can also derive from loving behaviors aimed at protecting the other partner from facing his or her fears or dealing with "what lies beneath." It happens when one partner gives in to fears or surrenders the responsibility to manage these fears to the person he or she loves. One example is the younger wife who is drawn to the idea of a man who takes care of everything, and so she surrenders her responsibility for many matters to her older husband. While it may seem like one partner is solely responsible for how things are done in the relationship, the other partner is equally responsible for creating this dynamic. In the example of the older husband and the younger wife, it could be that the husband fears that who he is won't be enough for his younger wife, and so, maybe without meaning to, he pushes his wife into a childlike dependency on him, which, he believes, will guarantee her loyalty. (This husband is similar to those individuals who can't seem to stop dating fixer-uppers: an underlying issue causes them to make themselves needed to the point where they could never be abandoned.)

In the Parent Trap conflict loop, and all the other conflict loops in this book, it takes both partners to create this dynamic. Only when you look at the payoff for both sides can you alter this dynamic and bring the relationship back into balance.

I know, I know. As you're reading this, you might be thinking to yourself, *Yeah right! If only my partner would step up, get things done right, and show some backbone, then I would treat him or her like an adult!* Or you might be thinking, *Heck, if my partner is going to micromanage every second of my day, I might as well just sit back and let my partner do everything him- or herself!* But if you're going to move from the Parent Trap conflict loop into the Equal Partnership circle of love, it is absolutely essential to understand that half of the responsibility is yours. Right now it may feel scary or even impossible to push back against the set of boundaries in your relationship and test your assumption of what would happen if you "stepped up" or stopped micromanaging, or simply to start acting like you were in an equal partnership. But you owe it to yourself and your partner to challenge the status quo. What would happen? Would nothing get done? Would the mechanics of your day-to-day lives fall apart? Would "acting like an adult" mean walking straight into even more conflict than the relationship is exhibiting right now?

Not only is challenging these beliefs essential for your relationship, but freeing yourself from the unfair label of "parent" or "child" can help you live a more authentic and full life. This is one time among many in this book when you have the opportunity to use your relationship as a forum for personal growth. If you stopped being the parent or you stopped being the child, what are you afraid would happen? It's time to challenge this fear.

CHILDISH VS. CHILDLIKE

A few years ago, I was standing in line at Peet's Coffee in Sea-Tac Airport. SFO was fogged in, and I was on the phone, telling my husband, Eric, that I would be home late. When I hung up, the woman next to me in line caught my attention.

"Excuse me," she said, "but aren't you Dr. Tara? I recognize your voice from the radio."

I turned to find a woman in her early forties, with perfect nails and hair, wearing a tailored suit. It turned out we were on the same delayed flight.

"I'm Susan," she said and then got to the point. "I know you must get this all the time, but do you mind if I run something by you?"

"Not at all," I said.

We grabbed our lattes and found a quiet corner in the airport.

"First off," said Susan, "I want you to know that I love my husband, Stephen. We've been married for five years, together for eight, and we have a beautiful three-year-old son, Ethan. But I find that I always have to be the grown-up in the relationship, and I hate it. Honestly, I'm relieved that my flight's delayed, because I know that as soon as I get home, I'll be walking into some kind of disaster."

"What kind of disaster?" I asked.

"Well, the boys will be having a great time, but the house will be a wreck—toys everywhere, no food in the fridge, laundry still in the washer—and I'll have to clean it all up." She explained that maybe Stephen would fold some of the clothes, but not the right way, and that he'd do some of the dishes, but he'd leave the dirty pots in the sink. "I'm the CEO of a tech company. I work long hours, and I'm responsible for a lot of people's jobs. It would be nice to come home and not always have to be in charge there, too."

I let Susan keep talking, and eventually she brought the conversation around to sex. When I asked about her sex life with Stephen, she laughed. "Ha! What sex life?" she said. "He says he's not turned on when I treat him like I'm his mother, and I can't get turned on by a little boy." She paused to sip her coffee. "Look, it feels like I've got two kids at home instead of one. I miss that strong, sexy man that I married."

I see this all the time in my practice, regardless of the individuals' gender or sexual orientation. One partner becomes the caretaker of the other, and over time the pattern becomes so entrenched, it's as if one is parenting the other. It doesn't feel great on the flip side, either. On the child side of the Parent Trap, it feels as if you are constantly being told what to do and how to do it. *Nagging* is such a negative word, but that's what my clients say it is all the time.

On one side is all the responsibility; on the other side is a get-out-of-jail-free card of no responsibility, at the price of the person's autonomy. Those in the child's role say, "Well, sure, why even try? I'll never get it right," and they sit back and watch their partner take care of everything, but this comes at the price of being a balanced team. What starts out as something small—just a little imbalance in one partner's sense of responsibility and the other's accountability—if not explored and remedied, builds into a conflict loop that destroys the love that is there. The Parent Trap also destroys whatever sexual passion is there. Like Susan said, who wants to have sex with someone who is childish, and who wants to have sex with someone who reminds you of a nagging parent?

While the roles of the Parent Trap don't always fall along gender lines, I do tend to see more women slipping into the role of parent and more men slipping into the role of child than vice versa. This may hinge on how our brains are wired or how we're brought up. Based on research conducted by Gijsbert Stoet and colleagues, women are better multitaskers than men. The female ability to keep many balls in the air all at once and the male ability to laser focus on one task from start to finish may not be expressed in all cases, but it's expressed in most. In a relationship, this can look like a woman answering work e-mails while helping the kids with their homework, washing a load of whites, and whipping up a healthy weeknight dinner all at the same time, while the man walls himself off from the multitasking chaos by picking one thing to focus on and putting in figurative earplugs against everything else. Sometimes I'll be walking through the house on the way to my home office and I'll think, *Hey, why don't I just walk into the laundry room and throw in a load of laundry on the way and miss the first pitch of my beloved San Francisco Giants?* But when my husband heads into the living room to watch the game, he makes it there without taking a detour. And often I envy this about him!

Sometimes my multitasking means that I never even

make it to the home office; on some occasions I don't accomplish what I set out to do, because I can't resist multitasking my way into being completely sidetracked. But my husband always gets that one thing done, and done right. And, God love him, sometimes I want to say, "Hey, honey!" as he walks right past that latest load of laundry that needs folding. These are two equally valid ways of being, but when one partner's behavior doesn't meet the other partner's expectations, the Parent Trap that results can wear on the relationship.

From Susan's description, it was obvious that she and Stephen knew they were stuck in some sort of pattern in which she was the foreman and he was the assembly line worker, but they didn't know what to do about it. Stephen did some of the housework, managed some of the couple's calendar, and scheduled an oil change pretty much when the car needed it, but he just didn't do those things the "right" way. In order for Susan to have things done in a way that gave her peace, she felt like she had to do them herself.

For his part, Stephen didn't really care how the laundry was folded or if the car got detailed at the same time they changed the oil, and he was willing to humor Susan only so far. Eventually, he threw up his hands—it seemed as if nothing he did could ever live up to Susan's standards, and so he quit trying. Stephen's conclusion was that if he couldn't do it right, then why do it at all?

Susan told me that she didn't want to relax her standards, and that rather than repeatedly going over the ways things needed to be done, it just seemed easier to do them herself. She complained that Stephen didn't participate, but behind her words was the idea that when Stephen did participate, he messed it all up. And there they were, stuck in the Parent Trap.

The thing is, with this conflict loop, and with all the others in this book, we can look from outside the relationship and see pretty clearly that Susan could loosen up her standards and Stephen could choose to make a greater effort and not use Susan's perfectionism as an excuse. But from inside the conflict loop, it can feel like there is no way out. Susan bossed Stephen around not because she wanted to, but because she thought that she had to. If she didn't stay on top of things, it felt like a disaster was going to happen, and so she was doing whatever it took to avoid this disaster. And Stephen avoided taking care of Susan's honey-do list not because he was incompetent or spiteful, but because trying was the quickest path to failure. So often in a relationship, our thoughts and actions are deeply impacted by our and our partner's opinions of how things are done compared with the way things should be done. We say, "If you loved me, you would . . . "

So where do these points of view come from?

As Susan and I continued chatting in the Seattle airport, our talk gradually turned to her childhood. Both of her parents had had high-powered jobs and often worked late. It fell to Susan, the eldest of four children, to pick up the slack. "I became the mom," she said. "When things in the home were chaotic, I felt chaotic. If I didn't wash the dishes or fold the laundry or pick up after everyone, it just didn't get done." Once, while Susan was on the phone with a girlfriend, her youngest sibling climbed onto the kitchen counter to get herself some cereal, fell, and broke her arm. No wonder Susan had so much anxiety! The one time in her life when she loosened her grip on control, there really was a disaster.

But just as Susan's past had conditioned her to seek control, it had also made her seek a man who could help her relinquish it, at least in the beginning of their relationship. See, Susan had fallen in love with Stephen's ability to have fun, be adventurous, be spontaneous—so many of the things she had missed out on in her childhood. Here's what you really want to keep in mind: so many of your partner's qualities that you fell in love with early in the relationship—the things you really wanted more of—can become the very things that you feel the most critical about and end up rejecting or even killing off after years spent together.

At the beginning of their relationship, Susan loved the way Stephen made her feel: he could make her laugh, help her be spontaneous and a little more easygoing. He was childlike. He was playful, full of wonder and curiosity, and even a little dangerous, ways of being that Susan had never had a chance to experience herself. But what she had once seen as childlike, she now saw as childish. Every time she saw a stack of dishes in the sink or a load of laundry in the wash, all those old fears about chaos came rushing right back to her, until she was bracing for imminent disaster. Inside of her was the young girl who wanted to talk to her friend on the phone, and that girl was competing with the eldest sibling, who was in the parent role and who saw the consequences of torpor. And the eldest sibling was winning. Susan couldn't notice what Stephen did right, including being a loving, attentive father, because she was overwhelmed by the expectation of disaster whenever she noticed the many things he did "wrong."

"Let's fix this," I said.

When SFO is fogged in, it can be really fogged in, and so we still had some time on our hands. I offered some suggestions, some 3-Minute Fixes, that Susan might want to try.

3-MINUTE FIX

CHALLENGE YOUR FEAR

Susan feared that if she didn't stay on top of things, there would be a disaster. But would there really? We saw how Susan created this expectation, but now it was time for a closer look.

"Is this your fear, or is it a real fact in the here and now?" I asked her.

It's time to ask yourself the same thing. Look inside your relationship to discover what you fear. If you surrendered control or let your partner just be, what do you fear would happen? Is the feeling or the situation you envision familiar? Notice that it's not about figuring out your partner. It's about figuring out things about yourself. For many couples, the Parent Trap is reinforced by fear—fear of looking "bad" to an outside entity if your household isn't "perfect"; fear of missing things or falling behind; fear of the unknown, which, it seems, can be kept at bay by regimentation. *What is your fear?*

It may take some time, but once you have identified the fear at the root of your behavior, it's time to challenge it. Ask yourself what would really happen if your fear came true. Might that visiting parent feel a little more at ease if your living room looked lived in? On the other side, if you tried to live up to your partner's demanding expectations for a week, maybe there wouldn't be as much conflict as you think. Susan worried that when she came home, the house would be a disaster, but deep down she knew that Stephen and Ethan would be sitting on the floor, playing a game and having a great time. I challenged her to join them. *How can you challenge your fear?*

3-MINUTE FIX

A DAILY DOSE OF GRATITUDE

Most relationships start in a loving circle in which we melt at the wonderful things we love about our mate. And then, little by little, we stop noticing these things and start noticing the negatives. It becomes a bad habit. Over time our brains are literally rewired to see what they are doing wrong instead of what they are doing right. We focus on the things we dislike about our partners instead of those things we used to love and, on some level, still long for.

You always hope that once you find your way back to this circle of love, you will start noticing these wonderful things in your partner again. But what you have to do is choose to consciously seek out these things again; they will lead you back to that circle of love. Don't play the "When, Then" game, waiting to feel love before taking loving action! Start taking the action now, and love will follow.

Every day list five things you appreciate about your mate. They could be small things . . .

the fact that she remembered to pick up your dry cleaning
that wonderful sandwich he made you for lunch

Or major things . . .

the college fund he started for your kids

the time she spent on the phone, haggling with an insurance company

Share your gratitude face-to-face, scribble your sentiments on a Post-it and stick it on the bathroom mirror, or send a thank-you via text. You can even compile a list in a Gratitude Journal. And don't beat yourself up if some days you can come up with only one or two compliments for your list. The important thing is not to miss an opportunity to show your spouse or partner some appreciation.

It's amazing how many precious moments we let slip through our fingers, those times when we think to ourselves, *Oh, that is sweet,* but we don't say anything to our partner. Yet we always, *always* have a comment ready when our partner says or does something we don't like. Next time you're feeling appreciative or loving, grab on to that moment. Text him or her, e-mail, or walk over there and give him or her a kiss.

Susan's first gratitude list, which she scribbled on the back of a napkin in the airport, looked like this:

I really appreciate it when it's a beautiful star-filled night and you take my hand and say, "Close the computer, honey. Let's go outside."

You help me have some fun . . . and that's not easy.

I love it when you bring me coffee and give me a kiss on the forehead.

When I start believing that my whole sense of self is based on my career, you never fail to remind me of the things that are more important—strong friendships, volunteering, the things I bring to the world and to our relationship.

Three weeks after our airport encounter, I got an e-mail from Susan:

> Just wanted to say thank you for your help! We did what you said and tried a new activity together: salsa dancing! I was worried about the steps, but Stephen was so great. When I went into my head, he was tuned in to me and really noticed. He just looked in my eyes and said, "Focus on me. You're doing great. It's all about having fun!" You know what? It was about more than having fun. I had forgotten about his ability to not judge himself and how it could help me be a little less judgmental of myself, too. I was sweating, and he said, "Just put your hair up!" So I did. I know I didn't look good, but I felt great. It was such a turn-on, in a way I hadn't felt in years. And let's just say the night ended well. It felt so good to be with the man I love.

UNSPOKEN EXPECTATIONS

The other day I was loading my dog into the car to meet my friend Nikki for a hike just north of San Francisco. We'd been hiking together pretty frequently, especially since Nikki had turned fifty and was doing some soul-searching. She had been a senior oncology nurse and had worked in that field since her twenties, but she had become aware at fifty that she was suffering from compassion fatigue and totally burned out and needed to do something else— something that had the kind of meaning that nursing used to have for her. This "something else" was still a little bit up in the air, but Nikki had been talking about offering vegan cooking classes. "After years in oncology, I want to do something that addresses the cause, not the cure," she had said. "And I never want to be in a hospital setting again."

We'd had the same hiking plan the previous week, but Nicki had called to cancel while I was driving up to meet her. She and her partner, Shannon, had had a big blowup. Shannon and Nikki had been a loving couple for a decade, and I could tell that whatever Nikki had canceled for was important when she asked me if I could recommend a couples counselor.

Now I was on my way to meet her again, and I looked forward to seeing her and hearing what was going on. There was Nikki's car, parked at the trailhead. *Phew!* I parked next to her, and as we started to walk, she began to tell me what had happened.

"Well, you know, everything came to a head last week, as I was leaving to meet you," Nikki said. It turned out that Nikki had been telling Shannon that she was going out to work on putting together her new career. She had said she was planning the cooking classes, building a new website, having meetings with people who knew the field, and doing other business stuff, when in reality, she wasn't ready to do any of that yet. Nikki had erroneously believed that by not telling Shannon her truth—that she needed time to heal and repair and connect with her friends—she was protecting Shannon from the anxiety of uncertainty. The reverse was true: her strategy had created anxiety in

Shannon, but for different reasons. For Shannon, an alarm had started going off—she didn't know what the issue was, but something wasn't right. Last week, Shannon had checked Nikki's odometer, read a couple of texts, and realized that instead of working on a new business, Nikki had been seeing friends.

"I think she thought I was having an affair," Nikki said.

Nikki and Shannon had since been to see my friend Tim, an excellent couples counselor whom I had known for years. As an oncology nurse, Nikki had been the couple's primary breadwinner for years. Though Shannon had finally settled into a steady job, she was terrified that Nikki's new career wouldn't work out and that they wouldn't be able to make ends meet. Nikki told me that in the session with Tim, Shannon had talked about her fear of what she called "becoming a bag lady, pushing a cart somewhere." Nikki was nervous about her new career, too, but she knew Shannon's fear was much stronger than her own, and she had tried to protect her from this stress and uncertainty by making her business seem much more concrete and definite than it was.

Of course, as soon as Nikki started bending the truth, Shannon knew something was up and started keeping track of her. Lies begot lies, and what started as "I'm just running out to do a little research," when Nikki was actually taking the dogs to the beach, grew into the Parent Trap. Nikki became like a teenager rolling the family car out of the driveway in the middle of the night, and Shannon became like a parent, keeping tabs on her partner to catch her in the act. (Nikki was also "gaslighting" her partner—downplaying or denying the truth of Shannon's perceptions—but we'll get into gaslighting much more in Chapter 5.)

In the safety of the therapy office, Nikki was able to be authentic and tell Shannon her truth—that Shannon wasn't nuts, and that Nikki hadn't been planning her business. She had a sense of what she wanted to do, but she just wasn't ready and had been afraid to share her uncertainty. By not being honest with her partner, Nikki had created the very thing she believed she was protecting against, making Shannon more anxious. Nikki admitted to the specifics of sneaking out to play while texting Shannon that she was hard at work on her business. Shannon admitted to spying and checking up on Nikki. Nikki exhibited emotional courage, one of the 3 Secret Ingredients for a Lasting Relationship—it took emotional courage on Nikki's part to tell the truth, not just the truth of what she had been doing, but also her inner truth that she needed time.

"We kind of laughed a little bit," Nikki said as we hiked. "I realized that while I thought I was protecting Shannon, I was really protecting myself, and by not being honest with her, I was missing an opportunity to acknowledge these fears that were holding me back and to grow together with Shannon."

Nikki and Shannon were caught in the Parent Trap conflict loop. Nikki saw herself as the primary breadwinner (the adult) and Shannon as someone who was not mature enough to handle the truth (and thus was essentially a fearful dependent, a child), which led to an imbalance of power and responsibility in the relationship. Whether you're fighting about household chores or money or a lack of responsibility and respect, this pattern usually stems from a combination of deep-seated fears and an ensuing battle for control. Nikki knew that taking time off to transition, connect with friends, and go for a hike would activate Shannon's fears. So Nikki did the thing that was easiest at the time—she lied to Shannon, hoping to avoid having to deal with the short-term conflict that the truth would create. But in the long term, Nikki created exactly the conflict she was hoping to avoid.

Also, deep down, Nikki didn't believe she had the right to tell Shannon that she didn't want to pursue traditional work for a while, that she wanted the freedom to figure out what to do next. She worried about appearing selfish, lazy, irresponsible, or entitled. She was too afraid to express and acknowledge her real feelings, both to Shannon and to herself.

Luckily, Shannon and Nikki were not in their conflict loop for all that long, so perhaps it was easier for them to come clean in their session with Tim and admit their lies (on Nikki's side) and their spying (on Shannon's side). While Nikki and I hiked that day, we talked about what would help them move forward and avoid falling into the same conflict loop again. It wasn't as if Shannon's fear of "becoming a bag lady" had evaporated when Nikki came clean, and it wasn't as if Nikki was willing to give up her dream of a new career or jump right into it immediately after their session with Tim.

I am constantly reminding my clients that when you can approach your partner from a place of curiosity rather than a place of judgment, the thing you're fighting about tends to fade away and the loving behavior follows. When Nikki and Shannon approached their conflict loop from this perspective, they realized that the fuel for their conflict was the difference between their expectations. Shannon expected Nikki to start her new career immediately; Nikki needed time off to recover and refuel before moving on to the next chapter in her life. When Shannon saw that her expectation wasn't being met, it felt to her like Nikki might never start her new career. Nikki realized that she wasn't doing herself or Shannon any favors by sneaking around, that by withholding her truth, she was depriving herself and Shannon of an opportunity to grow, to get in touch with and repair unexplored wounds or false beliefs that had been holding them hostage. It was courage that Nikki had been lacking when she was sneaking around. When Nikki finally communicated her plan, she and Shannon were able to understand each other's expectations and adjust their own expectations accordingly. Nikki was able to reconnect with herself and with friends, while transitioning into a new life that would feed her soul, and Shannon felt assured that Nikki was working toward building a new career.

When you take the time to face your fears and approach your partner's expectations with curiosity, you create more love and preempt conflict.

ARE YOUR FEARS HOLDING YOU HOSTAGE?

Several pages ago, with Susan and Stephen, we saw how important it is to challenge the fears that form the backbone of a conflict loop. For Susan, this was the fear that something disastrous would happen if she stopped "checking up on" Stephen. In the case of Nikki and Shannon, there was another fear in place: Shannon's fear that without Nikki's financial contribution, they would end up broke.

Are your fears holding you hostage, as Shannon's was? Here's a chance to explore the truth of these fears. Ask yourself the following questions to start discovering if your fears match reality:

1. What are the fears you entertain and the beliefs you adhere to that make it impossible for you to be authentic and truthful with your mate?

2. What do you think will happen if you challenge those fears and beliefs by taking action? (Free-associate here. Write down what comes to mind, even if it sounds crazy.) You might think, *My partner just couldn't handle it.* But couldn't they? Really? What do you get from letting your partner make those vacation reservations or take care of the mortgage? What's the payoff if you let your partner take charge? How does it benefit you to stay in your role?

3. What is an action you can take to confront those fears? If you have slipped into the parent role, could you stop "giving instructions" for one morning and see what happens? If you have slipped into the child role, could you plan a weekend activity without being prompted (or nudged or nagged)? List at least two actions you

can take to break out of your role in the Parent Trap, take a deep breath, and act on them. What do you have to lose?

3-MINUTE FIX
♥

SHARE EXPECTATIONS

Nikki's and Shannon's previous behaviors stemmed from a source of conflict that many couples find themselves negotiating: they just assume their partner knows what the plan is. The misunderstanding in the plan can be something as grand as thinking you're going to have two children in the near future, when in actuality your partner wants to wait, or it can be as small as the expectation that your partner will make two cups of tea in the evening, when in fact he or she plans to make only one cup. Couples get themselves into trouble when they don't articulate their expectations.

Your partner cannot know what's in your heart unless you have the courage to tell him or her, and you cannot know if the fears you're harboring about your partner are legitimate (maybe Shannon really wouldn't have understood, and maybe she'd have tried to end the relationship) unless you have the courage to face them. In "The Owner's Manual," chapter 8 of this book, are questions that can help you explore the big expectations—those about children, religion, family, politics, and more—that form the backbone of many relationships. In this 3-Minute Fix, take time to examine assumptions and expectations that are specific to your relationship. Ask yourself the following questions:

1. In your relationship, what is one thing you're not being com-

pletely truthful about? This doesn't have to be a "lie." It can be something like withholding how you really feel about how your partner spends money or takes care of his or her body or communicates with friends and family.

2. What do you fear will happen if you are completely truthful about this aspect of your relationship?

3. Are you willing to confront this fear and see if your expectations are on target?

BREAKING THE HABIT, ONCE AND FOR ALL

Maybe you've promised yourself that you'll never, ever get caught in the Parent Trap again. But no matter how courageously some people fight to extricate themselves from a relationship in which they have fallen into the role of parent or child, and no matter how much they swear it will never happen again, these roles can be so comfortable. It can be so easy to sink back into the same Parent Trap conflict loop in a new relationship.

That's what happened to Phil and Leah, childhood sweethearts who were separated when Leah's family moved away and who now, decades later, were both divorcés. Leah was a strong woman with a master's degree in English, but in her previous marriage she gave up her power little by little to a controlling husband. Eventually, her first husband gave her an allowance and said things like, "I pay the mortgage," which kept him in control and kept Leah dependent on him. With her youngest daughter months away from going off to college, Leah made the choice to take back her power, restore her sense of self, and find her way back to the woman she used to be. Leah started divorce proceedings, determined to live the second half of her life with dignity and respect.

Phil had done something similar. His first wife wasn't happy. Phil ended up letting himself become solely responsible for her happiness so that he could squelch his gnawing fear that she would become unhappy enough to abandon him. After they divorced, Phil made a commitment to himself: he wasn't going to allow his fear of abandonment force him to be *solely* responsible for the emotional and financial well-being of his next partner.

Let's rewind a little bit. Way before these first marriages, Phil and Leah had lived in the same neighborhood and had dated when they were thirteen. Then Leah's family had moved, and they never really saw each other again. They were each other's first loves, a powerful force that can pull at the heartstrings even decades later. After his divorce, when Phil had been single for about a year and had just endured another bad blind date, he started thinking about Leah. He went on Facebook to try to track her down and to see what had happened to her after all this time. There she was—with two grown kids, in the middle of a divorce. She was living a couple of states away. When Phil reached out, Leah admitted that she'd thought about him, too, sometimes and about what could have been. They started reconnecting, and the cloud of her first marriage started to lift from Leah's heart.

But she was also overwhelmed. Working out the divorce settlement, selling the house, and handling her kids' feelings and her own felt like a reenactment of the Greek myth of Sisyphus, who was condemned to roll a boulder up a hill every day, just to have it roll down every night. Phil was an attorney at a successful law firm, and he wanted to help. He swooped in, pushed back against Leah's ex-husband, took over the paperwork, and even helped get Leah's youngest daughter off to college. It felt good! Phil felt valued in their relationship; Leah felt like she had found her knight in shining armor. They met for long romantic weekends. For both of them, finding their way back to each other after all those years was like a dream come true.

Their long-distance romance lasted a year. Leah remained overwhelmed, and Phil wanted to make everything as easy as possible, wanted to protect the love of his life, who was in a stressful and complicated life transition—especially because it was in his nature, and was an essential part of his profession, to take care of exactly these kinds of details. While Phil helped take care of things, Leah was able to focus on being excited and hopeful about the possibility of having a second chance with the person she had fallen in love with so many decades ago. When Leah agreed to move in, he arranged everything, down to the plane ticket and the movers. Finally, all the fires had been put out. All that was left was to live the fairy tale. But once the doing was done, what was the fairy tale going to look like?

Phil happily plugged himself right back into his life, his routine, which was now even better thanks to the addition of the most important part: Leah. He would go off in the morning and perform his job. Leah looked around and, without the distraction of the "doing," found she was a stranger in a strange land. Suddenly the space didn't feel like hers. Maybe she just needed to redecorate? Maybe then she'd feel more at home? She started repainting rooms, buying new linens, rethinking some of the furniture. Leah was dealing not only with an empty nest, having seen her last child off to college, but also with a completely new nest altogether. To manage all the complicated newness of her life, Leah filled herself up by buying things to feather the new nest and frenetically working to make it feel like home. Leah fell into a trap that so many women find themselves in: she tried to fill the void from the outside, when really it was an inside job.

Then the bills started rolling in. At first, Phil just looked at them and paid them, but before long things got out of control. Here was a bill for five thousand dollars and then another for seven thousand dollars. Little by little, Phil fell back into the role of "Daddy," and Leah slipped back into the role of a child with an allowance. As much as they had wanted to create a new kind of partnership, Phil and Leah had slipped back into the same Parent Trap pattern they had made a conscious effort to retire. Phil saw what was happening and made an appointment with me, which is how he and Leah ended up in my office.

"Why didn't anyone bring up how much money was being spent?" I asked after they filled me in on the particulars.

"She gave up so much by coming here, I didn't want to say no," Phil said. "And I want her to be happy."

Here was another great example of short-term gain at the expense of long-term pain. Neither Phil nor Leah wanted to take on the conversation of her spending—they avoided the conflict that sitting down and hashing out a budget might have created. Fortunately, they had the maturity to recognize that their fantasy wasn't matching their new reality, and made the choice as a couple to work on it. What would have taken a pinch of emotional courage to rectify a couple of months ago was now going to take a bushel of emotional courage. Fortunately, these two had a rock-solid commitment to each other and to doing things right this time. For Phil and Leah, it was mostly about awareness—once they realized that they had fallen into the Parent Trap, and especially when they saw the loving actions and the vulnerability that had started this conflict loop (Phil's desire to ease Leah's transition, and Leah's need to "fill herself up" after a stressful year), they were ready to get down to business.

I let them know that I had complete confidence in the beautiful foundation they had created together and that I respected the life lessons they had learned in past relationships. They weren't playing the blame game, and they were open and willing to look at their blunders. Both Phil and Leah wanted this one to be for keeps. Still, it was so easy for them to slip back into their toxic but familiar roles.

"It sounds like the next step is to really talk about our money—what we have, how to set it up," Leah said.

"Sounds great," said Phil. "Even talking about how we spend money is something I never would have done with my ex-wife."

I said, "I love that it was your idea, Leah, to set up an appointment with a financial planner, which shows you've already moved out of your child role and into that of the intelligent, capable woman you know you are."

Do you remember the case of Nikki and Shannon, and how their Parent Trap grew out of the difference in their expectations for how Nikki would spend her time after quitting her job? Setting a budget is another way to communicate expectations. As long as both partners' voices are represented in the budget, it's a way to agree on what they expect in terms of their finances. By formulating a budget, they are saying to each other, "Here's how much we can spend and how we agree to spend it." But setting a budget wasn't going to heal what ailed Leah, what made her feel she needed to spend money.

"The second part is that it sounds like you have to start building your life here together as a 'we,'" I explained. As exciting as it was for Leah to embark on this adventure with Phil in the second half of her life, it meant that she had to leave her old life behind, including her support system, her routines, and some of the things she used to do to make herself feel good. As much as Phil meant to her, he couldn't be responsible for all of Leah's good feelings. Nor did she want him to be. But if they were going to work together as a team, it was important to communicate and discover how they envisioned their life together and how they could support each other as they both evolved as individuals and traversed the next stages of life together, hand in hand.

We continued to talk, focusing on activities that Leah enjoyed and brainstorming about how to incorporate them into her new life here with Phil. "You know, I go by these dog parks, and it looks like such a nice community," Phil said at one point in the conversation. "I know you said you always wanted a dog, but your ex was allergic. What do you think about stopping by a shelter and taking a look? Maybe a new ritual for us can be going to the dog park after work."

As we focused on Leah's activities, the conversation turned to Leah's desire to go back to work. She mentioned that instead of teaching English, she might move to teaching creative writing. "Maybe I'll take a look at that jobs board over at the community college," she said. Phil remarked that he could go online with her and even drive to the community college with her and help her take a look around.

"Here's what's so beautiful about this," I said. "It's like a new beginning in two ways. It's not just the romantic story of first loves reunited, but the two of you together are getting a second chance at having a healthy, interdependent, loving relationship, one that can help you each come into your own, be the person you really want to be."

Leah took Phil's hand. "I really am happy that I'm here and that we're together."

Leah and Phil were both committed to their new partnership. They had the emotional courage to confront an all too familiar conflict loop that was taking shape. And they had hope. Together, Phil and Leah had the 3 Secret Ingredients for a Lasting Relationship. They just needed to know how to use them.

THE POWER OF LEARNING SOMETHING NEW TOGETHER

We're conditioned to think that when our feelings change, we'll take an action, but the reverse is often true: when we take an action, the feelings will follow. No, it doesn't have to be sex (though if the mood strikes, it's not a bad idea). Based on research conducted by Arthur Aron and colleagues, couples who learn an activity that is new to both of them strengthen their relationship and create a deeper bond. Trying any new activity can help you get out of the mental ruts of your old way of being. And who knows, this new activity might become one of your favorite rituals together. The activity doesn't have to be exciting or extreme; it could be something as simple as learning to make sushi together. Especially for couples like Phil and Leah, who have amassed so many individual experiences during lifetimes apart, it can be important to start creating new, shared experiences together.

Take some time and make a list of activities or experiences that you would love to share with your partner. For example, your list could include hiking the Grand Canyon, trying an exotic food, watching a new-to-you movie, and sitting at a group table at a restaurant instead of in your usual isolated booth. Make the list really long and then share your ideas. Now pick a couple of possibilities from your partner's list while he or she picks possibilities from yours. With openness and curiosity, choose one activity to try first. But if agreeing on just one is too difficult right now, then pick one from each list. Try these activities with an open mind and a good spirit.

HEARTwork

Transforming the Parent Trap into an Equal Partnership

Exercise 1: The Parent Trap Quiz

Are you and your spouse or partner stuck in the Parent Trap conflict loop? To find out, read the following statements, and for each one, circle the number for the response that comes closest to how you feel.

---

1 = Strongly Disagree, 2 = Disagree, 3 = Agree, 4 = Strongly Agree

1. I feel frustrated when my partner doesn't do his or her "fair share" around the house, or I feel disrespected when my partner doesn't acknowledge my contribution.

   1   2   3   4

2. If I surrender control to my partner, things won't be done right; or my partner is so exacting that I feel like I can't ever do things in a way that meets his or her standard.

   1   2   3   4

3. I feel like my partner doesn't respect what I can do.

   1   2   3   4

4. I feel like my partner's "vote" counts for more or less than mine when we are making a decision.

   1   2   3   4

5. I always have to nag, or I'm always being nagged.

   1   2   3   4

6. One of us is always reminding the other to eat right, exercise, get a physical, or otherwise take care of him- or herself.

1	2	3	4

7. I hate it when I have to speak for my partner or when he or she speaks for me.

1	2	3	4

8. One of us is a micromanager.

1	2	3	4

9. Sometimes I feel so resentful that I do things just to piss him or her off.

1	2	3	4

10. What I used to find so endearing about my mate now makes me cringe.

1	2	3	4

11. The person who makes more money has more power.

1	2	3	4

12. My partner is so uptight or so footloose that I can't stand it.

1	2	3	4

13. My partner is childish, or it seems like I'm being parented in my relationship.

1	2	3	4

14. My partner is a neatnik or a slob.

1	2	3	4

15. My partner tells me what to do at all times or has unreasonable expectations that I will keep track of what we're supposed to do at all times.

    1   2   3   4

16. One of us does almost everything, while the other does almost nothing.

    1   2   3   4

17. One of us has way more leisure time than the other.

    1   2   3   4

18. One of us spends way more pocket cash than the other.

    1   2   3   4

19. It's my job to remind my partner of things on his or her to-do list (e.g., have a physical by the end of the year or pick up the dry cleaning), or it's my partner's job to remind me.

    1   2   3   4

20. One of us is so childlike that it crosses the line into "childish."

    1   2   3   4

Scoring: Add up the numbers you circled for your total score.

Below 35: It's unlikely that you and your partner are in the Parent Trap. Most of the time, you work together as a team. You may split work, responsibilities, or power, but however you divide things up, it works for you. Feel free to move on to the next chapter. You may relate more to one of the other four conflict loops.

35–50: While you and your spouse or partner may not be caught in a full-blown Parent Trap, you are definitely exhibiting some of the symptoms. Keep in mind that this pattern often grows more extreme over time. Continue on to HEARTwork exercises 2 and 3, which should help get you back on the path toward the Equal Partnership circle of love.

51 or above: You are almost certainly stuck in the Parent Trap. Continue on to HEARTwork exercises 2 and 3 to start creating the type of equality and balance that makes for a strong, healthy team.

Exercise 2: Acknowledge Your Part in the Pattern

Partners stuck in the Parent Trap conflict loop often spend a lot of time complaining about their partner's behavior ("If he would stop acting like such a child, I wouldn't treat him like one"), but rarely do they acknowledge their own part in the pattern, that is, the payoff or secondary gain they reap. For example, if you're in the child role, you might be kvetching that you have no power, but there's a payoff: if you don't make the choices, then you're not responsible for the consequences if things don't work out. The person in the parent role gains, too: it may be hard work, but being in charge means you get everything your way. This exercise is the time to be honest with yourself, even if you're not yet ready to share these feelings with your spouse or partner.

That said, some mothering or fathering in a relationship can be very healing and nurturing, so don't throw the baby out with the bathwater. Again, it's all about finding what works for you. It's only when the division of power and responsibility feels wrong or is a turnoff to your partner that you've got a problem. If that is the case, consider the payoff to you (look really deep down inside) of keeping your spouse or partner in the parent or child role, and then complete the following statements.

I may be reinforcing my spouse's parent/child role by_____

_____

I am protecting myself from feeling_____

_____

If I stop this behavior, my fear is that _____

_____

Exercise 3: Reframe the "Child" and "Parent" Roles

Some of the characteristics you once loved about your spouse or partner may now be the very things that create conflict. You might have loved how spontaneous your partner was when you were dating . . . but now this behavior just seems flighty and irresponsible (childlike); or you might have loved your partner's reliability and ability to ground you in the present . . . but now your partner just seems boring (parental). The descriptors "parent" and "child" have their negative aspects within the framework of an adult relationship, but they also have positive aspects. The following exercise is designed to help you reframe the way you view these roles in order to help you find your way back to the circle of love, where the positive aspects of the roles you and your partner play take precedence.

If you identify as the parent in your relationship:

Choose an activity that your partner enjoys and is good at, preferably something that you think you could learn to enjoy, too. It might be mountain biking or cooking or playing the guitar—it doesn't matter what it is. Just choose something that he or she can teach you, and then let him or her do just that. You've been in the role of teacher, supervisor, foreman, and general leader long enough, so spend some time learning from your partner. Why? Because this is a natural way to force a move toward a balance of power, which is one of the many great advantages of creating a bond.

If you're stuck in the parent role, you can often forget that your partner has valuable skills, knowledge, and expertise to contribute to the relationship. Often we make the healthy choice of picking a mate who can bring the qualities and skills we wish we had more of: exhibiting patience, being good at figures and numbers, organizing, cooking, expressing feelings. You don't have a monopoly on expertise! But learning from the "child" in the relationship forces the dynamic to change, and simply experiencing this new dynamic and seeing that it's possible can have a lasting effect on the relationship.

If you identify as the child in your relationship:

Choose something about which your spouse or partner is usually controlling or rigid or "parental" in some other way and find a way to embrace it. Is your spouse particular about packing the trunk before a long trip? Is your partner particular about maintaining the financial records? Rather than fight him or her on this, work toward appreciating the outcomes. Hey, you get a tightly packed trunk and meticulous financial records! Though giving away too much responsibility and control results in the Parent Trap conflict loop, learning to appreciate the skills your partner brings to the relationship is a step toward the Equal Partnership circle of love.

Here's a great example of how one couple embraced their differences and used the parent-child dynamic to their advantage. I have a long-term client, Stephanie, who is very particular about the storage of her pots and pans. Every time her husband, John, put something away "incorrectly," they would fight. One day John decided there had to be something he could do about this.

After dinner he said, "Honey, does everything look the way you would like it to be?"

She said, "Yes."

He took out his iPhone and snapped a picture, and one weekend while she was away, he made a storage area in which each pot and pan fit perfectly, exactly as Stephanie wanted. Instead of continuing to fight with Stephanie about the placement of the pots and pans, John reinterpreted her position as an opportunity to have an organized kitchen. By embracing this aspect of Stephanie's "parent" role, John was able to show his competence, and Stephanie was able to appreciate his impressive carpentry skills.

Not only did John's actions provide a really simple solution to the problem, but they also created peace. The couple had been fighting about who was right and who was wrong, and John decided, *Why don't I just fix this?* Let's admit that this took emotional courage. What if Stephanie didn't like what he'd done? What if she hated the new kitchen organizer? But John took the risk and came up with this great left-brain fix. Stephanie later told me that it was, hands down, the most wonderful and thoughtful gift she had ever received. It wasn't about the storage for the pots and pans (though the new setup certainly made after-dinner cleanup a snap). It was the meaning behind it. John's gift showed that he really got her, and John experienced joy from how happy he had made his wife.

In your relationship, is it all the small things that add up to a home filled with tension instead of love? A friend of mine calls this phenomenon "death by a thousand needles." One way to unravel this tension is to pinpoint a behavior that you know causes friction and then, with no expectations, just change it. Maybe it's taking your shoes off before you walk in the house or not texting, even if it is a business matter, when you are in the middle of a conversation with your spouse or partner. This is the kind of thing you could waste time and resources on by processing it in therapy . . . or you could just change the behavior. What loving action can you take right now toward appreciating, even celebrating, the differences between you and your partner?

Chapter 4

• • • • • • •

Come Close, Go Away ∞
Interdependent Relationship

IMAGINE A TUG-OF-WAR. You're gripping one end of the rope, and your partner is gripping the other. Between you is a pit of mud. And you're both pulling as hard as you can, straining your muscles, your minds, and your emotions to knock the other person right on his or her tush and drag him or her through the mud over to your side. Winning means pulling until the other person falls down. Losing means giving up and getting dragged through the mud. This is the Come Close, Go Away conflict loop. Unfortunately, in this tug-of-war, no one ever wins. You can't exist as a slave to your partner's needs, and as much as you keep fighting to haul your partner over to your side, and into your way of understanding, that's no way for your partner to live, either. And you know that you both can't keep pulling forever.

I'm here to tell you there's a third option: If you both ease up on the rope equally, the flag will stay centered. Once neither you nor your partner is pulling on the rope, you can lay it down. Eventually, you can walk away from the rope completely. In your heart of hearts you know that it's going to take stepping away from your ego for you both to end up as winners—with the love that you want.

Maybe you know why you and your partner are pulling. Maybe you started gradually, and now it's been so long, you can't even remember what started the war. But now it feels like you can't stop. At least that keeps the flag sort of centered between you, right? As with all the scenarios in this book, it takes emotional courage to be the one who starts to ease up first. You have to trust that when you look down the rope and into your partner's eyes and practice loving behavior by unclenching your jaw and leaning in just a little bit, your partner will do the same. Taking that one-way ticket out of the Land of Me and making yourself vulnerable to your partner is the only way the relationship has a chance. If you continue pulling, you will remain deadlocked or one of you will win. Either way, the relationship loses. So why not take a chance and be the one to make the first move?

Now comes the part where we get to identify and explore just what kind of Come Close, Go Away tug-of-war you are in. There are four scenarios:

- You are both afraid. One of you fears abandonment, while the other fears being smothered. As one of you tries to come close, the other retreats.

- Both of you are afraid of being vulnerable and exposed, warts and all, to the other partner, making you both pull away from face-to-face intimacy.
- You and your partner have different expectations about closeness and what it means to be partnered, making one of you expect the other to "come close," while the other sees this approach as an attack and feels trapped and engulfed.
- You and your partner have different expectations about sex. Some of us need to feel emotionally connected to our mate before we feel open and desiring of sex, whereas others use sex as a way to create the emotional connection that is lacking. With this emotional catch-22, there's not going to be a whole lot of lovemaking going on anytime soon!

In all these versions of the Come Close, Go Away conflict loop, a partner pulls away from the person at the other end of the rope. The partner who needs reassurance is matched with the partner who needs space; the lover who uses sex to feel close is matched with the lover who has to feel close in order to have sex; the person who pursues a string of unwinnable trophy dates is matched with a person who thinks that beneath her trophy exterior she is unlovable, damaged goods, or somehow defective, or as my best friend, Harley, says, "not fit for human consumption."

If you are the partner who pulls away, perhaps you are doing what it takes not to be "found out." Maybe you endured the emotional devastation of a parent's abandonment, and you learned to protect yourself from rejection by beating your lovers to the punch. Or you were told you were not good enough over and over again, until you started to believe it, and now you can't let anyone come close enough to see what's under the mask you wear. Now you can't help but act according to the behavioral patterns you have created. You keep your partner at arm's length, or desperately try to pull him or her closer when your fears are tapped into, until you feel a sense of safety, albeit a false one.

On the other side of the rope, you might think that if you let your partner cross that intimacy threshold, you will never be yourself again. Maybe in past relationships you stretched your heart wide open, only to have it shattered, and so you told yourself, *Never again!* If you keep your partner at a distance, you'll never lose yourself; if you don't get too invested, you can't be hurt. Are you willing to challenge that belief now? Are you willing to make a new choice?

These conflicts spring from some of our most basic needs as humans. We want safety, we want acceptance, and we want love. But sometimes the ways we learned to earn or safeguard this acceptance, safety, and love while we were young or in a previous relationship don't have the same effect in our current adult relationship. Sometimes these old behavioral patterns need revision. What created these patterns? Do they still serve their purpose?

In all these cases, it's more than a one-person problem. So before going any further, make the commitment to see yourself, as well as your partner, in these pages. Move forward with the intention to understand your partner with an attitude of openness and curiosity, and most importantly, withhold judgment of your partner and yourself.

A relationship provides an opportunity to receive love and acceptance from another person and, most importantly, to create a safe space for you to discover yourself. As you seek to get to the bottom of the tug-of-war in your relationship and move toward an Interdependent Relationship circle of love, sometimes gaining a simple understanding of why your partner does these things that frustrate you can be enough. Sometimes knowledge of past events that contributed to your partner's behavioral patterns, and some empathy on your part, can help you both stop the tug-of-war.

The following sections will guide you through the evaluation process.

MAINTAINING THE "ME" IN "WE"

"Look, I'd like to go fishing with my buddies this weekend. I really don't see the problem," Jake said. He and his wife of six months, Caroline, were in the middle of yet another heated discussion about "quality time." Jake crossed his arms, visibly frustrated.

"No way," she said, shaking her head. "We have a million projects going on at the house, and besides, we're so busy, we never get any 'us' time."

"Even when I'm at work, we're having 'us' time! I can't even go to the bathroom without texting," Jake said.

Caroline wanted a connection, but Jake needed his space. As she tried to get close, he kept saying "Go away!" The problem got so bad, they came to see me.

"I feel like I never have time for myself, and between that

and the constant need for updating, it makes me lose sight of this beautiful woman I love," Jake told me. When he heard his wife's ringtone, Jake said he felt like his body was being "pulled on," and he was "gasping for air like a fish in a boat."

Caroline closed her eyes and remained quiet.

Managing "me" time and "we" time is a tricky balance for many couples. But the issue goes beyond time. I see so many couples who struggle to find the right balance of emotional togetherness. How much of their identity is created by the relationship, and how much is created by being an individual person? When couples can't find a middle ground between the need to be together and the need to be apart, both physically and emotionally, their circle of love can devolve into the Come Close, Go Away conflict loop. One partner reaches out for a connection and desires togetherness, while the other retreats, afraid of losing him- or herself in the relationship. This only encourages the partner who needs a connection and reassurance to pull harder, and the retreating partner to retreat further. The pattern becomes more and more entrenched over time.

As we sat together in my office, Jake and Caroline on opposite ends of the sofa, I asked Jake to close his eyes, take a breath, and describe exactly what he was feeling in that moment. He explained that he felt anxious and annoyed. He said he just wanted to "get away."

"Have you ever felt that kind of urgent need to run away before? Is the feeling familiar?"

"Well, yeah," he said, thinking. "It reminds me of my mother."

Jake's mother had been a single parent. With no close

family and no close friends, Jake's mom had turned to him and had made him her confidant when he was as young as nine. She had talked to him about her feelings, her problems, her hopes, and her relationships. She had literally cried on Jake's shoulder and had asked young Jake to help her through some hard times. He had been her little man. Sometimes, Jake said, he had felt as if his mother's entire day was centered on waiting for him to arrive home from school. He had felt responsible for her happiness. If she wasn't happy, he'd feared it meant that he wasn't doing his job as her son.

"That sounds like an awfully big job for such a little boy," I said.

Jake nodded.

Healthy parenting supports and nurtures kids, and effective parents help their kids manage their emotions so that they can someday manage them on their own. But with Jake, the roles had been reversed and the support had flowed in the other direction. He had been thrust into the inappropriate role of an "adult child." He loved his mother, but her actions had taught him to sacrifice his needs in favor of hers.

Jake realized that he was afraid that if he allowed Caroline to get as close as she wanted, he would become so enmeshed in her concerns that he would lose himself in her, just as he'd become engulfed by his mother's needs when he was a child.

It is healthy to be a "we"—to be able to move as one with your partner, to be a couple, to be a team in the world. But it's also important to hold on to who you are as an individual and to be able to keep growing as a person. "Can I be a 'we' and also maintain who I am outside of the relationship?" is a valid question. When this "me" in "we" gets out of balance—or when it's been out of balance long enough—some people assume that the only way to be themselves again is to bail on the relationship. The challenge and the opportunity is to learn to flow in and out—to allow yourself to merge with the other person, while also being able to separate and be yourself.

In a healthy relationship the partners have the ability to flow in and out of the relationship without the fear of enmeshment or abandonment, and to clearly separate the past from the here and now. Problems arise when one partner feels that there needs to be more togetherness, more "we," or conversely, more space to be an individual, more "me." Even more challenging is when one partner wants the other to abandon parts of him- or herself—in the form of other relationships, activities, or beliefs—or when one person freely gives up these things, expecting the relationship, and the new identity as a "we" within the relationship, to take the place of everything that defined him or her as an individual. The real challenge, both as an individual and a couple, is to formulate who you are as a couple while at the same time retaining, and even adding to, who you are as individuals. Maybe it's keeping your Wednesday night basketball game but going to the farmers' market as a couple. Or taking a long weekend to go to a yoga retreat with your girlfriends, but reserving Thursday night as your date night.

In my office that day, as we delved deeper into those

actions that were causing friction between Jake and Caroline, Jake slowly began to make a connection. Every time Caroline called him at work and asked when he would be home, or discouraged him from spending time alone with his buddies—every time she tried to pull him close—all those old feelings from childhood came rushing right back.

"It's not that I don't want to spend time with Caroline," he said. "It's just that I need some time by myself, to be myself, too. I want to know that I can go fishing and she won't feel rejected. Or that I can blow twenty dollars on a poker game and have a cigar with my buddies without Caroline perceiving it as a betrayal. I want that confident, capable woman I fell in love with."

The room was silent for a few moments. Finally, Caroline said, "You know what, honey? I think I get it."

"I want you to," Jake said, reaching out and taking Caroline's hand.

"I know you have talked before about how suffocating your mother could be, but I didn't realize what a profound effect it had had on you, and my heart goes out to that little boy."

This is the transformative thing about having the emotional courage to open up in front of your partner. Listening to Jake talk about his childhood not only helped Caroline understand her husband, but it also helped her realize for the first time that his pulling away wasn't about her. Interestingly, this new understanding between them gave Caroline exactly what she wanted: Jake moved closer to her. But as he moved closer, Caroline began to pull back. We were both curious about what was going on with her.

She started to talk about her father, who had left the family when she was seven. "He'd make plans to see me, and he wouldn't show. He promised vacations that never happened," she said.

I asked Caroline about her first marriage. She shared for the first time that her previous husband had been a serial cheater. She looked at Jake. "I know you've never given me a reason to mistrust you . . . but still!" she cried.

Though it wasn't something she could easily put into words, Caroline felt that some part of her had made her father leave and that this same part had made her first husband cheat. As Caroline continued sharing the details of her first marriage, she explained that she had given her previous husband quite a bit of space—space he eventually used to betray her. On some level, she'd sworn that she would not repeat this mistake. No wonder she wanted to draw Jake closer: her fear of abandonment was triggered every time Jake began to withdraw. She felt like infidelity was bound to happen again. If Jake didn't check in during the day, it meant he wasn't thinking about her and didn't love her, and any day now he would betray her, just like her father and her first husband had.

This is why Caroline and Jake were caught in the Come Close, Go Away conflict loop. His fear of being too close was triggered by her fear of abandonment, and, of course, Caroline's fear of abandonment was made worse every time Jake tried to pull away. Because of Caroline's past, she expected Jake to act in a certain way—if she gave him space, he would cheat and leave. And because of Jake's past, he expected Caroline to act in a certain way—if he let her in, she would take and take and take, until there was nothing left of him. Both Jake and Caroline were unwittingly holding each other responsible for painful wounds from the past and transgressions by those who came before.

But now Jake understood that Caroline's wounds from the past were fueling her need for reassurance. And Caroline knew why Jake needed space. With this newfound understanding, everyone was able to breathe for the first time. Having this pattern on the table in front of them allowed Jake and Caroline to become aware of the dynamic and understand it together.

"Let's explore this a bit more," I said, turning to Jake. "Can you think of some ways in which Caroline is like your mother? What do the two of them have in common?"

Jake hemmed and hawed before answering. "Well, actually, I . . . I can't," he stammered. "Not really. Caroline is kind and generous. She's a loving, happy person. She's usually smiling. In a lot of ways, she's the opposite of my mom."

"Isn't this a wonderful moment of awareness?" I said, turning to Caroline. "Can you list some ways in which Jake is like your ex-husband?"

"I see where you're going with this. And you're right. They're nothing alike. Jake and my ex are totally different."

At this point in the conversation, Jake was holding Caroline. They were actually having the experience of intimacy they had both been yearning for. And what was really beautiful was that their combined empathy for each other's experiences was stronger than the conflict itself.

"Now how are you feeling about the fishing trip?" I asked Caroline.

"I'm . . . happy he's going," she said. "I'm thinking how wonderful it is now to have a husband I trust. And you know what? I have a couple of girlfriends who keep saying they haven't seen me in forever, and this might be a nice opportunity to change that."

"And I know that I'll enjoy the fishing trip, but I'll also look forward to coming home—coming back to our marriage and to the woman I love," Jake said.

Now Jake and Caroline were able to look at each other with fresh eyes, without distortion from relationships that came before or the baggage from their pasts. Now they were able to be in the here and now, instead of being held hostage by fears. The beautiful thing is that with this new empathy and this new understanding of each other's pasts, the events that had created the need for space or the need for reassurance—what the couple had been fighting about—ceased to matter altogether. Whether or not Jake went on the trip wasn't even an issue anymore. Now with a foot back inside the Interdependent Relationship circle of love, Jake and Caroline could see a relationship in which there was both "me" and "we"—a relationship they could flow in and flow out of, secure in the knowledge that the marriage would always be there when they returned. Caroline wanted to support him in being happy, and Jake couldn't wait to come home to her.

3-MINUTE FIX

♥

TRANSITION TIME

Jake felt like the second he walked in the door after work, Caroline would pounce on him and hand him a list of stuff to do that she had been ruminating about all day. Caroline felt like she was meeting him with openness. She was so happy he was home, and she wanted to share her day. He had spent the day as a "me," and then he had to turn on a dime and instantly become a "we" when he got home.

It's hard to make a split-second transition from office manager to attentive husband or from office manager to bedroom goddess! In fact, I've had countless clients—men and women—admit that they sometimes take a later ferry, sneak off to the gym, or delay coming home in some other way for fear that they'll be pounced on as soon as they walk in the door. Sometimes, we need a moment to be a "me" before we're ready to be a "we."

I know this from my own marriage. Even though we live in California, Eric's job runs on an East Coast schedule, which means his workday ends at 2:00 P.M. By the time I come home around 8:00 P.M. he's already had six hours of alone time, so he's done his "me" thing and is ready to be "we." As blessed as I am to have a husband who welcomes me with open arms, I still need time to decompress—to change into comfy clothes, wash my face, and putter around for a bit after a hug and a kiss. Once I've had fifteen minutes to shake off the day, though, I'm ready to catch up, pour a glass of wine, and start making dinner together. What could have become a conflict for us is now a healthy ritual. These days if I walk in the door and launch right into a conversation, he'll remind me to change my clothes and get comfortable first.

Ask your partner, "Hey, do you need a little space when you come home from work?" Or maybe you or your partner wants some space after the kids have gone to sleep. Figure out where you and the person you love need a little space, and then put a time limit on it. Maybe it's two minutes, maybe it's ten, or maybe it's half an hour. Most of us can handle anything as long as we know when it will be over. So if you need half an hour to catch up on baseball scores or friends' Facebook updates, or forty-five minutes to hit the home gym after work, just make sure your partner knows when "we" time will begin, and most importantly, what the agreed-upon time frame is for an activity. This is especially essential if you have been in a Come Close, Go Away conflict loop or have issues around abandonment. There should be no restrictions on and no judgments about how a person uses this "me" time to transition. Whatever your partner chooses to do during transition time, give him or her the space and the freedom to do it.

CAN YOU LOVE WHAT LIES BENEATH?

I recognized Francesca from the cover of fashion magazines long before I met her in person. She was even more stunning close up, with her big brown eyes, full lips, and curvaceous figure. She had just turned thirty and had come to therapy because she wanted to figure out why she always ended up with men who were either married or didn't admit they had a girlfriend, even when she asked.

Francesca spent a year with me, exploring her fears in individual counseling. She told her agent she wanted to cut back, and then she took a hiatus from work and dating to discover what was important to her. I remember in her first session with me, she told me she had fat thighs.

"I usually dim the lights before I look in the mirror," she said. She teared up a little, but then I watched her shut her emotions down and regain her composure. She apologized for being such a downer and sat up straight, a pleasant smile plastered across her face. Here was this drop-dead gorgeous woman who had been considered for a while the most beautiful woman in the world, and she couldn't even look at herself in the mirror! I was stunned and felt an overwhelming sadness for her. My first thought was, *What has been done to you to make you feel this way?*

Remember *The Rules,* the bestselling dating guide from the nineties? The book claimed to have figured out the secret to making men want you: never accept an invitation to go on a date on Saturday later in the week than Tuesday; use an egg timer when speaking on the phone with a potential mate, keep the call under two minutes, and always be the one to end it; be mysterious and play hard to get; and grow your hair long and never wear pants. It was, to put it bluntly, a manual on how to be inauthentic. The book could have been written by Francesca's mother, Rose.

Rose was the daughter of poor Italian immigrants. As soon as she saved up enough babysitting money, she dyed her hair blond. Later, she had her nose done. Slowly, Rose had molded herself into a prize, and then she set her sights on landing a well-bred, Waspy husband. She eventually married a man—Francesca's father—who fit the bill: rich, successful, and all-American. Their wedding was straight out of *Town & Country*, and the guest list made Page Six of the *New York Post*. Rose was married in a replica of Grace Kelly's iconic dress.

A few years later, Francesca was born. Her extended Italian family was overjoyed; her mother, however, was not. That's because Francesca looked, well, Italian, with her enormous brown eyes and a full head of curly brown hair. By the time Francesca turned twelve, Rose set out to change that: she had Francesca's eyebrows thinned and her hair bleached and straightened. (Luckily, Rose's attempts to surgically alter some of Francesca's other features were thwarted by ethical plastic surgeons.) By the time Francesca turned sixteen, Rose was parading her in front of elite New York modeling agencies. She encouraged Francesca to put off college. "Modeling first. Then you can go looking for a husband," she said. But when Francesca followed her mother's lead and found success as a model, Rose was fiercely jealous. Francesca's dad might as well not have existed, and any love he gave Francesca had to be dished out on the sly . . . or he risked Rose's wrath.

Listening to her story, I thought about how far from the truth Francesca's beliefs about herself really were. Francesca was smart, loving, and deeply vulnerable, in addition to being beautiful.

After dating a string of wealthy, successful men, Francesca had her first "real" relationship with David, an Oscar-winning producer who at just thirty-four had a net worth close to a billion dollars. He cheated on Francesca and then reeled her back in for three years. "What do you expect?" Rose asked her. "Men will be men!"

A couple of years ago Francesca started adopting stray and unwanted pets, bringing home every one-legged, half-blind, bucktoothed dog she could find. At a fund-raiser for a local pet sanctuary, Francesca agreed to auction a date with herself. Michael was the highest bidder. One date became more. Michael was the first man Francesca had dated who wasn't in "the industry." He was a pediatrician who volunteered for Doctors Without Borders and loved stray dogs, too. He was kind and present, and he pursued her madly. He made it clear that he wanted to make a commitment, and in true *pursuer* form, he jumped through whatever hoops he could to make this beautiful yet elusive woman commit to him.

They dated for a year, and recently Francesca thought Michael could be the one, and she decided to stop acting as a *distancer*, keeping him at arm's length, and to open up, be vulnerable, and let him in completely. She finally told Michael that she loved him. And that was when things started to go wrong. Suddenly Michael became distant and evasive; he began canceling plans and even avoiding her phone calls. Now Francesca was working through why Michael had suddenly pulled a disappearing act. "What am I doing wrong?" she asked me during one of our sessions. She also confessed that she found herself wondering what David, the producer, was up to these days.

We all have fears and insecurities. We all worry that if we reveal our authentic self, warts and all, our partner will go running for the hills. But for some people, like Francesca, these anxieties can spin out of control—she believed that something about her was fundamentally flawed, that she was, at her core, unlovable and unworthy of love. Here's where things get really tricky: Without being aware, many people do a great job of selecting the perfect partner to reinforce these beliefs. They pick a partner who lets them keep believing these things about themselves. For Francesca, David was the perfect partner in crime; he reinforced every message Francesca had ever heard from her mother, such as that she wasn't good enough and that deep down there was nothing to love.

If you grew up in a family like Francesca's—if you were taught to believe that your appearance or the size of your paycheck defined you—you might be drawn to narcissistic partners like David, too. You might subconsciously go looking for that man, or woman, who was really focused on appearances, or control, power, and status; someone who casually offered to pay for your hair coloring or your nose job or compared your yacht to the other, bigger yachts at the marina; someone who didn't care about who you *were* as a person, just how you appeared at first glance and on paper.

Francesca met Michael after she had spent a year in therapy and had worked on developing a healthier sense of self after her experience with David. Her relationship with Michael was the first one that Francesca had had that wasn't built on image alone. But the minute she stopped letting her mother's approach to relationships control her actions—the minute she stopped distancing herself from Michael and tried to be a little more authentic—Michael seemed to lose interest. Self-doubt started to creep in. *Had her mother had been right all along?* she wondered.

Eventually, I asked Francesca how she would feel about

having Michael join us for a session, if he was open to the idea. The couple came to my office a week later. As we spoke, Michael revealed that he was a born achiever—a straight-A student, the star of his high school tennis and track teams, the winner of a full ride to UCLA (from which he graduated magna cum laude), and now a respected pediatrician in the Bay Area. Despite his successes, however, he had never gotten any real recognition from his parents.

"If I missed a shot during a tennis match, my parents would give me that look," he said. "I'd have my photo in the local paper, and I'd barely get a 'Good job' out of them."

"But you kept trying to win them over?"

He nodded.

All Michael had ever known was the chase, the relentless pursuit of "success," whatever that meant at any given moment. Now that he'd won his latest "prize"— Francesca—he didn't know what to do with it. Like so many couples I see, Michael and Francesca had initially found themselves in a relationship that allowed them to be who their families and their past experiences had trained them to be: Francesca could be distant, while keeping her true self hidden, and Michael could go after her like a greyhound chasing a rabbit.

But now, after we had been working together individually for so long, Francesca was committed to being her authentic self and could risk the rejection her ego and her mother had conditioned her to believe would result if she let her true self be seen, warts and all. Her readiness to challenge herself by being open and present in the relationship threatened to undermine the whole foundation it was built on. Ultimately, the relationship provided both Francesca and Michael with the opportunity to abandon the patterns that had defined their lives, to put their old beliefs under the microscope. This Come Close, Go Away conflict loop was the perfect place for Francesca to challenge the belief that beneath those stunning looks was an unlovable person and for Michael to challenge the belief that he was defined by his achievements, the trophies on his shelf.

Francesca found herself at the crossroads we had been working toward for so long. She finally had the chance ask herself whether she would be lovable if she were completely present and exposed what she saw as her vulnerability. You can ask yourself the same questions Francesca asked herself: Are you willing to reveal your authentic self, every last part of your being, which you have kept so well hidden? Are you willing to find out whether the notions that you have been conditioned to believe, and that have taken you hostage, are true?

At that session with Michael, Francesca struggled to discuss a very painful memory and went back to her habit of smiling while holding back tears. She had yet to cry in front of Michael, at least during couples counseling. I asked her what was going on, and Michael encouraged her, saying, "It's okay. Tell me."

"No, no," she kept saying over and over. Michael reached out and tried to hold her hand, but she pulled away from him. She was crying now, curling into herself while gesturing with her hands, as if to say, "No, no!"

"You know this isn't about you, right?" I said to Michael.

Michael nodded. "Yes," he said. "My heart is just . . . breaking for her."

"Would you let him come a little closer to you?" I asked Francesca.

"I'm just a mess right now," she said.

"Not in my eyes," Michael said. "When I see how you are with your rescue dogs, the never-ending love you have for them and your determination to find them just the right home, your courage to turn your back on a career that so many women would kill for, because it's not right for who you want to be—that's why I love you. That's why I can't get enough of you."

"Francesca," I said, "do you want to tell Michael what you admire about him?"

She said that she loved Michael's decision to pursue a career that was meaningful for him, that she admired the fact that he had found the courage to diverge from his parents' plan of being a superstar neurosurgeon, and that it was nice that he loved his work in a family practice and his humanitarian work.

"I love the fact that you truly accept me for who I am. And it's been good for me to see your courage in going your own way, as I'm trying to do the same," she said.

Michael moved closer to Francesca. When he wrapped his arms around her, she let him. With mascara running down her face and her bare feet tucked under her, she smiled. They officially became the couple I knew they could be. Michael started individual therapy. A couple of months later they were back in my office again . . . this time for premarital counseling!

3-MINUTE FIX ♥

BE HERE NOW

If you're in the Come Close, Go Away conflict loop, you probably have a pretty good idea who tends to seek distance and who tends to pursue. Think about it. How do you pursue or create distance from your partner? What are the things you do? Now ask yourself if you're willing to stop doing those things and just experience whatever it is that happens in their place. Are you willing to discover the outcome of being authentically present with your partner? Do you wish to find out that you can be loved for who you are?

3-MINUTE FIX ♥

A DATE AU NATUREL

What do you feel you have to do in order to be liked or loved? Do you hide the truth about your background, make sure your clothing is perfect, or feel like you have to impress with hard-to-get reservations at restaurants?

Here's your chance to challenge that belief: Pick one of these "surface" things that you think is crucial to being loved and try going on a date without it. I'm not saying that you should stop bathing or brushing your teeth, or that you should trade being charming for being rude. But for just one date, let your natural self shine through the exterior you usually present to the world. Keep in mind that this exercise isn't necessarily about your physical appearance. If you believe that acceptance comes from the stuff you provide, try planning a date or an experience that doesn't cost any money. No fancy packaging.

Create a date that is rich with creativity and meaning. No matter if you are a man or a woman, a *distancer* or a *pursuer* in the Come Close, Go Away conflict loop, just for one date, let your soul and not your exterior do the talking. Revel in your true self: let your curls do their thing, speak up, and refuse to squelch your opinions, your sense of humor, or whatever you were told, and you decided, is unattractive, not feminine, or unmanly.

Even if it turns out that you like dressing up or going to fancy restaurants, for instance, going on a date without these things will prove to you that they aren't necessary. Who you are is enough, and it is likely that the very qualities that make you who you are also make you even more lovable, sexy, and attractive in the eyes of your beloved.

3-MINUTE FIX

WHERE YOU COME FROM

The reasons you feel unlovable or believe that your achievements speak louder than your self are probably rooted in your past. To figure out exactly what it was in your past that created these beliefs, you should endeavor to explore your childhood—and who better to explore it with than your partner? If you live close to where you grew up, take a trip together through your hometown. If not, look at personal photos and find some of your hometown online. As you drive or open the photo album, open up to and about yourself. Perhaps when you pass your grandmother's house or look at a photo of you and her together, you will remember baking cookies together and will recall how safe and nurtured you felt. Or perhaps as you drive by your old high school, you will share with your partner the story of how you got your heart broken by your first girlfriend. When you go by your old house, maybe you will you remember that closet you hid in when your parents were fighting.

Some memories will be happy. Some may be painful. But traveling back through your history, opening up, and sharing past moments, along with the feelings that accompanied them, with your partner is a way to understand where your behaviors come from and why you feel what you feel. Reliving these happy, sad, or even funny memories and allowing yourself to describe them to their fullest with the person you love adds depth to your relationship. If you are willing, use this experience as an opportunity to have the person who loves and accepts you validate those feelings, feel compassion, and create a new understanding. Give your partner the opportunity to say, "So *that's* why you start getting grumpy around the holidays." Give yourselves that opportunity to have a joint aha moment.

SEX AND THE "WHEN, THEN" GAME

One day a client told me it was his wedding anniversary.

"Mazel tov!" I said. "What are you doing to celebrate?"

"Well, nothing," he explained sadly. "All week I kept asking my wife if there was anything she wanted to do, and she kept saying no. So we're not doing anything. We've never really celebrated our anniversary, and now we've been fighting so much, what's the point?"

He was a young, handsome man, a six-foot-seven fireman who'd come to therapy to figure out what he could do about the couple's sex life. Since the birth of their second child, there hadn't been one.

Kara, his wife, was still nursing and told me in a later session, "I'm already a twenty-four-hour snack bar, and there's my husband, standing there, with that all too familiar look in his eye." The more Marco wanted sex, the more she pushed him away. "Marco will come over and say he just wants to hug me, just wants to be close," Kara said. "But you know what? Even when I like to hug him and kiss him, because I like that, too, I know that's just his quick foreplay. I know that a hug is going to lead us down a path I don't want to go down."

Eventually, Marco explained to me that it wasn't just the absence of sex that bothered him. "I'm lonely. I want my wife back," he said. "It seems like Kara's got time for the kids, time for her friends, time for her dance class. Just not time for me." It wasn't just that Marco wanted sex and felt neglected. He also felt rejected and minimized, like he'd been squeezed out of his wife's life.

As it is with a lot of men, when Marco wanted a close connection with his partner, he saw making love as the quickest pathway to create that connection. But one of the reasons Kara didn't feel open sexually was that she needed to have more of an emotional connection to Marco. For Kara and for many women, sex isn't just a physical expression;

it's an emotional expression, too. In the case of Marco and Kara, Marco wanted sex to bring them closer, but in order to have sex with him, Kara first needed to feel closer. I have so many couples who come into my office to work on this very issue: the men say they never have sex, and the women say they have sex all the time. I explain to them that men and women are at such cross-purposes when it comes to sex, it's really a wonder that they ever have sex at all. It can be such a relief for couples to find out that their sexual struggles are totally normal.

In this case, Marco felt that if he could only connect sexually with Kara, then their problems would disappear. But he had been trying for months, and nothing had changed: they had the same old request-and-deny conversation every other night. You can probably see that Marco and Kara are caught in the Come Close, Go Away conflict loop, but there's something else going on here, too. It's the "When, Then" game. Kara was sure that when she felt a stronger emotional connection to Marco, they'd start having sex again. Marco felt that if they had sex, then the relationship would be better. They were both looking toward the future, waiting for something to change as if by magic so that they could have what they wanted.

But here's the important part: they weren't really fighting about sex! Underneath this conflict loop, both of them wanted the same thing: a connection with their partner. They wanted that mix or balance of both love and a sexual bond. Sex was the symptom. The Come Close, Go Away conflict loop was the pattern, and the "When, Then" game made sure they stayed stuck in it.

For Kara and Marco, and for so many other young parents who have come into my office, there was even more going on—namely, sleep deprivation, which is a very real issue for new mothers. I can't tell you how many new moms have sat in my office and said, "If I have a choice between sex and sleep, I want sleep . . . please!" Over and over I have sat with couples with this problem. The new mother is desperately trying to get her husband to understand how exhausted she is—she feels disconnected from her body and is afraid of what the lack of sleep is doing to her mind. Then the new dad says he can't be expected to go without sex.

A problem arises when couples can't accept these natural changes and cope with them in way that creates a new, perhaps different, but even deeper love and bond. Some new fathers need a reality check: a new mom's sleep does take precedence. But this too will pass. If new fathers can stay out of the Land of Me for a while, the sexual relationship will return, perhaps even with renewed passion.

So now what?

As a fireman, Marco was overflowing with physical courage. But with his wife, he had the emotional courage of a bunny rabbit. On his wedding anniversary, a day to celebrate his relationship with his wife, he wasn't willing to risk the disappointment or the rejection that came with making plans to celebrate. What if he made dinner reservations and lined up a babysitter, and it turned out Kara didn't want to go? What if he put himself out there and Kara left him hanging? Instead, he wanted Kara to make it safe for him, to reassure him that if he made plans, she'd go along with them. He'd been asking Kara what she wanted to do so he didn't have to take an emotional risk.

"Besides," Marco said, "she's not feeling it. Why would we go out and pretend everything's okay?"

Man, this was one of the best examples of the "When, Then" game I'd ever seen! Marco was saying that when Kara felt it, then they could enjoy each other. But Kara was tapped out, depleted from being a snack bar, a jungle gym, and a cook, and there was Marco, just another person looking to take without giving.

"Okay, so you can either lick your wounds and complain about sex or you can step up and go after the very thing you have been complaining about. Your choice, my friend," I said. "She keeps telling you she needs to feel close and loved and cherished, and this is your chance! Are you going to blow it by playing the 'When, Then' game, or are you going to cowboy up and show some emotional courage?"

He sat there in silence, trying to figure out what to do.

I asked again, "So, what are you going to do for your anniversary?"

"Um, I'll buy flowers?" Marco said.

"What kind?" I asked.

He had no idea. He didn't even know if Kara liked flowers.

"She spends all day taking care of the kids. Then she doesn't have the energy to take care of you. Maybe do something that takes care of her?" I said.

"A massage!" Marco said. "She likes massages!"

"Then maybe dinner?" I asked.

He didn't know which restaurant was best, and he

didn't know if he could get a babysitter, but Marco liked the idea.

"Then what else are you going to do?" I asked.

"I'll . . . I'll write a card and let her know all the reasons I love her and what she means to me," Marco said. He started talking about all the ways he was going to express his appreciation in the card.

All of a sudden, Marco wasn't thinking about what his actions were going to do for him. He wasn't thinking about sex. His heart was open, and he was getting excited about the thought of making his wife happy. He had finally realized that Kara was "nurtured out." She felt like she'd been giving and giving and giving to their kids. The best way for Marco to come close was to nurture her in return. He felt good about contemplating what might make his wife feel open and nurtured. And he was getting excited about making it happen.

As in the case of Marco, the only way to stop playing the "When, Then" game is to say, "Now!" The words you say to your partner don't matter; it's really about your intention. Women can smell manipulation a mile away. It's about taking an action with no guarantees and no expectations in terms of what the results will be. It's about being in the present and finding joy in the process.

So if Marco took Kara out to dinner and expected sex afterward, or if he sent the kids to the park with a babysitter and then turned the lights down low, it would be just another instance of his coming close in a way that was bound to drive Kara further away. It would be asking Kara to fulfill his needs without respecting hers. And if Marco sent flowers to Kara, he would show a willingness to please her, but at the same time this gesture would prove to Kara that he had no idea what her needs were. Instead, Marco put his own desires aside and focused on pleasing his wife. The only thing he still needed was the emotional courage to follow through, and this he was able to summon.

"I couldn't get a babysitter," Marco admitted to me the week after his anniversary. "But I took the kids while Kara got a massage, and then we all went out to dinner."

Marco had learned why Kara had been retreating. He had figured out what she needed. He had relied on the 3 Secret Ingredients for a Lasting Relationship: intention, emotional courage, and hope.

"Tara, I'm telling you, it was the best date we ever had!" he said.

We worked to set up some new rules for the relationship, deciding, for example, that when Marco came home, there would always be a kiss and a hug. But in order for Kara to feel safe, she needed an agreed-upon boundary, a promise that the affection would not lead to sex. It was about creating more face-to-face intimacy and appreciating the sensuality of touch, both which satisfied their "skin hunger" yet remained separate from sex. This agreement let Kara enjoy the new ritual. Then we said that for the next thirty days, no matter what they were both feeling, they could snuggle and be affectionate, but there would be no intercourse—even if they both desired it. That month, Marco was able to start appreciating the touch of Kara's hand or just snuggling on the couch; and Kara enjoyed getting her feet rubbed and more of the kind of sensual kissing they had once spent hours doing when they were dating, before the kids came along, when there was time! A month of mindful affection and loving touch enriched Kara and Marco's physical and emotional connection and satisfied their skin hunger.

At the end of that month, after one of their standing date nights, not only was Kara feeling emotionally open, but she was also turned on, and she wanted to express her love and desire for Marco. "She was the one who was saying that the kids were asleep," Marco said, "and she was the one turning out the light."

3-MINUTE FIX

TAKING RISKS

Before you had a long-term commitment with your partner, you took big risks. Do you remember how scary it was to ask for a date? And, if you're married, do you recall how terrifying it was to ask for her hand or say, "I do?" Are you willing to take these same kinds of risks now? Or now that you're in the most important relationship in your life, do you play it safe? It's time to find the emotional courage to take a risk, like you used to. Plan a surprise activity—one based on your partner's likes and dislikes, not your own! Make sure to check the calendar and take care of other logistics (like a babysitter). Then take a risk and surprise your partner with an activity that he or she never saw coming.

3-MINUTE FIX
♥

CHORE PLAY: SUPPORT IS SEXY

An old "Dear Abby" column asked female readers which of the following would turn them on more: if their husbands did the dishes without being asked or if their husbands did a dance . . . naked. Something like 99 percent of readers agreed on the answer: Dishes. By a mile.

There's a time when respecting the differences between men and women can help a relationship in nine cases out of ten: during foreplay. I often tell my clients that for women, foreplay begins long before the lights go out. It starts when her partner cares enough to make an emotional connection and demonstrates an awareness of the things she needs most. Sometimes, it's offering to help around the house; other times, it's remembering to ask how that phone call with her mother-in-law went; and still other times it's giving her a platonic neck massage after she's had a long day at work. When a woman feels like her partner really knows her and cares for her, she begins to open up physically. Without that emotional connection, many women shut down sexually. Resentment builds. And for women, resentment is the number one killer of sexual feelings.

People will come to me and say that their relationship is on the rocks because of sex. I say that sexual issues are a symptom and not a cause. Once you've been to the doctor and eliminated the basic medical stuff that could be causing the problem—namely, medication, depression, and menopause—it's time for the partner who wants more sex to step out of the Land of Me, put aside his or her needs for a few minutes, and find the emotional courage to ask how his or her partner could feel heard, understood, and emotionally supported. Take some time to think about what you already know about your partner. Putting aside any agenda of your own (this is the most important part), what can you do to support your partner today? Now go and do it!

HEARTwork

Transforming Come Close, Go Away
into an Interdependent Relationship

Exercise 1: The Come Close, Go Away Quiz

Are you and your spouse or partner stuck in the Come Close, Go Away conflict loop? To find out, read the following statements, and for each one, circle the number for the response that comes closest to how you feel.

---

1 = Strongly Disagree, 2 = Disagree, 3 = Agree, 4 = Strongly Agree

1. I often wonder, when the wrinkles come and I start aging, will my partner still love me and desire me?

   1   2   3   4

2. I sometimes feel lonely, even if my partner is in the same room.

   1   2   3   4

3. I fear that over time I'm losing myself in this relationship.

   1   2   3   4

4. I need more or less "we" time.

   1   2   3   4

5. I think my partner is unreasonable about how much time he or she needs alone.

	1	2	3	4

6. When it comes to sex, I feel pulled on or I feel rejected. I wish my partner would initiate sex more or realize that sometimes it's just not the right time.

	1	2	3	4

7. When we have sex, it's like we're both going through the motions—like sex is a tool to reduce stress.

	1	2	3	4

8. I lie about how I spend my free time because I know my partner wouldn't approve.

	1	2	3	4

9. My partner tells me my body is just fine . . . but I don't believe it.

	1	2	3	4

10. I feel like I'm giving up myself to make my partner happy.

	1	2	3	4

11. My partner depends on me to make him or her happy.

	1	2	3	4

12. If it weren't for my body or my paycheck, I'd be single.

	1	2	3	4

13. My partner doesn't want me hanging out with my friends as much as I do.

	1	2	3	4

14. There's a power struggle in the bathroom: why can't we be in there together, or why can't he or she realize that even in a relationship, there's such a thing as TMI?

    1   2   3   4

15. Sometimes I pretend I'm busier than I am just so that I can get some alone time.

    1   2   3   4

16. I wish we could be affectionate without it always having to lead to sex.

    1   2   3   4

17. There's a piece of me that no one could love.

    1   2   3   4

18. We have different ideas about how often we should check in with each other during the day.

    1   2   3   4

19. Now that we're together, sometimes I wonder why.

    1   2   3   4

20. It's important to keep parts of ourselves secret. I mean, who wants to know too much?

    1   2   3   4

Scoring: Add up the numbers you circled for your total score.

Below 35: You and your partner already have an interdependent relationship, one in which you can flow together and flow apart, knowing that you each can take care of your own happiness but you're even better together. If that sounds like you, feel free to move on to the next chapter.

35–50: You and you partner are showing some warning signs of entering a Come Close, Go Away conflict loop. Continue on to the following HEARTwork exercises, which should help you reestablish a healthy balance between "me" time and "we" time and discover your and your partner's full value.

51 or above: Hello, Come Close, Go Away! Do you feel smothered? Do you worry about your partner's distance? If you want the relationship to last, changing these beliefs and this dynamic is essential. Get started by completing the following HEARTwork exercises.

Exercise 2: Find Fulfillment in "Me" Time

If you're unhappy, it's easy to blame your partner. It's easy to think, *If only I were with someone else, I would feel better!* But in a healthy relationship, *you* are responsible for fulfilling your own emotional needs. That's not to say that an emotionally fulfilling relationship won't help—naturally, you will be happier if you're more fulfilled. But it is not helpful, useful, or fair to make your partner 100 percent responsible for fulfilling your emotional needs.

If you're the *pursuer* in your relationship—the one who is most often trying for more "we" time and a closer connection—take some time to ask yourself the following two questions and jot down your answers:

1. What are three ways I can take care of myself when my partner is unavailable?
   For example, could you write in a journal, call a friend, pet the dog, go for a run?
2. How does it feel when my partner says he or she needs some space?
   Does it tap into an earlier time when you felt this way? What's the fear that surfaces when your partner needs some "me" time?

When you're ready, share your answers to these questions with your partner. Now carve out some time each and every week when you will commit to doing your own thing. Take some time to explore an activity or a hobby that gives you energy. Have you always wanted to join a book club, learn about electronics, start running? Ideally, during this time when you're doing your own thing, your partner will take some "me" time, too.

Exercise 3: Merge into "We" Time

Just as "me" time is important in any relationship, so, too, is "we" time. It's the balance between these two that creates a flow-in, flow-out *interdependent* relationship. If you're the *distancer* in this conflict loop—the one who most often pushes for time alone or time to do the things you love—here are some questions to ask yourself about your need for space. Jot down your answers.

1. What negative feelings do you tap into when your partner needs "we" time?
   Is there a fear of "losing yourself"? What does that mean to you? Do you believe that giving to your partner means "giving up yourself"?
2. What would happen if you trusted your partner completely?
   Do you feel like your partner would betray this trust?
3. What are three things you fear your partner would "discover" if you let yourself be known, warts and all?
   Do you think your partner could accept and love what he or she finds if you let yourself be "found out"?

When you're ready, share your answers with your partner. If you feel anxious or fearful about sharing your answers, share those feelings, as well. This is what being authentic means! Come up with weekly activities that you can do together, such as going to the farmers' market or to an open gallery walk, or sharing a favorite television show, which you can talk about later. Agree to check in with each other by exchanging little texts during the day. Decide how much "we" time you're comfortable with and the sorts of activities you would like to pursue, and then make this time together a priority. Don't cancel or reschedule unless it's absolutely necessary.

Chapter 5

• • • • • • •

The Blame Game and the Shame Spiral ∞ Ownership and Respect

B ACK IN THE eighties, the personal growth movement and certain schools of therapy said that if you're feeling angry, you should share it with the other person, just dump it on him or her, leaving the other person a mere puddle on the ground. This was supposed to help you release your anger. Maybe it even worked. Maybe it gave you a momentary rush of power and feeling of being in control. However, it was a quick fix that helped you feel better in the moment but that did nothing to address the wreckage you left behind.

If you are the recipient of the anger in your relationship, maybe you think that you're being a loving partner by letting your partner "get it all out" while you stand there, keep your mouth shut, and take it. But in this situation the loving action, one that will also ultimately help to strengthen your relationship, is being honest and having the emotional courage to say, "Listen, when you get angry like this, my heart shuts down, I want to distance myself, and I even start questioning the relationship."

In this chapter, you'll learn to refrain from dumping your anger on your partner or, conversely, to help your partner release his or her anger, and you'll master the art of letting your anger go so you can remove the barrier that the anger is creating. Underneath anger is almost always fear, pain, and/or terror over being vulnerable. Anger is a mask for these emotions, emotions you or your partner would otherwise have to feel.

You might say, "Can't I just get angry and get this off my chest so I can get to figuring out what is really going on?" Once you have a history together and confidence in your and your partner's intentions and ability to learn, grow, and take ownership, then in certain situations, such as in a therapist's office, and with your partner's permission and only with the intention of getting at what the anger is masking, you might allow yourself to get angry. (Keep reading. This chapter includes one of my favorite HEARTwork exercises to facilitate this process.)

But too often anger is employed to intimidate your partner into doing what you want. In other words, it's not a form of protection, a mask for fear or pain, but rather a tool for manipulation and control. When you angrily blame or shame your partner, you are trying to take power. Expressing anger is also a good way to ensure that you stay trapped in a conflict loop, rather than work toward a circle of love.

In this chapter we'll take a look at some examples of how partners in relationships have learned to look beneath anger and ask, "If I weren't feeling anger, what would I have to feel in its place?" And we will look at shame, blame, and anger as tools and forms of protection. Anger serves a purpose, and only by discovering its purpose in your relationship can you pack away the Blame Game and the Shame Spiral conflict loop in favor of the Ownership and Respect circle of love.

OY VEY: THE IN-LAWS

I was sitting in my office one afternoon, working on some notes, when my next clients rang the building call button. I buzzed them in, and the door opened down the hall. It was Bob and Carol, a couple I'd seen a few months ago. At the time they'd been having power struggles over his family, but she was pregnant and they'd just bought a new house, so they decided it wasn't a good time to dig into the work. Now they were back. Carol walked in front. Bob walked behind, with his face buried in his BlackBerry. He finished his text as they sat down at opposite ends of the room. It was pretty obvious they were locked down like Fort Knox.

"Welcome back," I said in my best soothing therapist voice. "What made you come back so soon?"

It was like the starting bell at the Kentucky Derby.

"I'm sick of having the same fight over and over," Bob said.

"You know what? Me too!" said Carol. "Who was it this

time?" she said, pointing at Bob's phone. "Your sister? Your mother? Your brother needs a place to stay? Are we supposed to chip in on a present for someone we don't know again?"

"There you go, ragging on my family again," said Bob. "And yes, that was my sister. I told you, they're all running a race this weekend, and they'll be crashing at our house to save time and money the next morning."

"Look, I'm glad this is all coming out in therapy, because this is so typical. They don't even ask me if it's okay if they stay over, nor do you. It is *our* home. And you know my best friend, Aubrey, is coming this weekend. I asked you, and we agreed about her visiting last week! And this is a rare occasion for her to be able to get away!" Carol yelled. "What did you text them back?"

"I haven't yet. I want to see how this session goes," said Bob. "Besides, this is ridiculous. Are we here to complain about my family or to talk about you and me?"

This is something all couples have to deal with: when you commit to a relationship with someone, you commit to a relationship with that person's family. There's no way your family is exactly the same as your partner's family, so there will inevitably be growing pains as you sort out your roles in this new, joined family. Furthermore, families are often a culture unto themselves. But when you begin to design your *own* family, it's easy to get caught up in false assumptions about the way things are "supposed to be," as if your family of origin's habits and traditions are the norm. Some people embrace their partner's family with joy, while others have a difficult time adjusting to the new family culture.

"Once he even left a restaurant when we were waiting for our food, to buy his father a card," Carol said, launching into another example of the impositions she'd endured. "By the time he came back, I had eaten and the food on his plate was cold. So much for date night! Then there's his married sister, calling every day with her latest psycho-drama, always sucking the air out of the room, looking for his advice about her stress. And then he gets off the phone, and he is wiped out, grumpy, irritable, and our evening is gone. We've been together four years, and his family hasn't even acknowledged me, not once," Carol said and turned to Bob. "Your mother comes over, and when I'm making dinner, she changes around the spices because, she says, *she* knows what you like!"

"What am I supposed to do?" said Bob. "I'm stuck in the middle. If you don't like it, why don't you tell her yourself?"

"Great. Perfect! There you are, setting me up to be the bad guy. You know what? When someone gets engaged or, heck, even when they're in a serious relationship, usually the family does something to welcome the newcomer. Forget a bridal shower or an engagement party, even a family picnic, whatever. I had a cup of coffee with your mom, and *I picked up the check*!"

"You're angry because they didn't throw you a party?" Bob asked.

"Argh! You don't get it! It's about acknowledging me, acknowledging *us*, and saying welcome to the family!"

"You keep saying that over and over," Bob said. "We keep fighting about the same thing. Just accept them the way they are, and get used to it. End of fight."

"The reason I keep bringing up all these things is I keep thinking it's like evidence. If you see what's going on, you will get it, come to your senses, and you'll stop caving in to all their requests, start setting boundaries with them, and maybe start putting us, our home, our life first," Carol said. "I keep bringing this stuff up, hoping that at some point you'll finally hear me."

"You look sad," I said to Carol when she was finished.

"No matter how I try with your family, it feels like I still haven't passed the audition," Carol said, addressing Bob. "I feel like I'm not important to you. Like if there was a choice to be made, you would choose them, not me. And then I'm responsible for the conflict."

"That's so not true," Bob said.

"But it *feels* that way," Carol said, turning to me. "I just feel like it's never going to work out, because at one point we're going to be fighting and they're going to win and he'll leave me for his family. I'm just really sad and scared."

There, finally, was the emotion the anger had been masking.

"What do you really want from me?" Bob threw up his hands in frustration.

"Can you ask that again?" I asked. "But in a soft and curious way. Because if you can, that's a really good question."

"What do you want from me?" Bob asked again, in a gentler voice.

"I want to know I am important, that when you say 'family,' you are thinking about me and our children, when we have them, first," said Carol. "It's just so different . . . so different than my family."

"In what way?" I asked.

"I was brought up to never impose," she answered. Then, glancing over at Bob, she said, "All they have done is show you how much they love you and accept you right from the first dinner we had. In my family I was always raised to wait for an invitation, and when you accept one, show up with arms open, a nice dessert, flowers, or a little gift."

"Tell me more about your family and how they have made the transition with Bob," I said.

"From the first time they met him, it was as though I was invisible, but in a good way. They were focused on finding out all about Bob, his family, his career, even what he likes. Since we have been together, they've been offering support, sending nice notes, stuff they think we could use for the house, and giving us both lots of emotional support, especially to Bob when he lost his job. My dad would tell him how much he believed in him. . . ."

"But . . . ," Bob said.

"But what?" Carol asked.

"What about your mom?" Bob answered. "All that is true, and I love your family. They treat me great, and I really like being with them . . . but they are not perfect. What about the way your mom treats you? No matter what you do, she's always critical. She always seems to have a reason to lose her temper with you, and you let her treat you in ways I know you wouldn't tolerate from anyone else. How many times have you gotten off the phone and burst into tears? You say you aren't going to just let it slide until she makes amends and things get talked out. That never happens, and you keep trying."

"I know," Carol said.

"Sounds like as different as your two families are, Carol, the role you have in both is pretty similar," I said.

Everyone has a role in the family they grew up in, and it's amazing how often these family roles help to shape who a person becomes as an adult. Bob would always be the family hero. That is why Bob's sister turns to him instead of to her own husband. By allowing his sister to remain so dependent on him, Bob wasn't really helping her connect with her own husband. And by being available to his sister so much, Bob was also missing out on opportunities to build a healthy and supportive relationship with his spouse. As far as Carol was concerned, it sounded like without some work, she might remain invisible in her marriage, just as she had been in her family while growing up.

I asked, "Carol, if you weren't feeling anger, what would you feel in its place?"

"Like I could disappear and he wouldn't even notice," she said.

"Like you feel at Bob's family gatherings?" I asked.

"How I sometimes feel with my own mother," she said. "No matter what I do, it is never good enough for her." She looked at Bob. "Now I am doing it with your family as well, but in a different way. I keep bringing your family gifts, keep showing up at all the parties to celebrate them, listen to them talk about themselves, hoping to win them over. Otherwise, I would go right back to being unseen and unimportant. I would be invisible, never good enough." She took a deep breath. "When does the audition end, Bob?"

"What, am I supposed to disown my family?" said Bob.

"No, of course not," said Carol. "I have always wanted more family, especially since most of my closest aunts and uncles have passed away. But when I am with your family, it is more painful than when I am alone. The real pain is that you just go into a trance when they call or you are with them and then . . ." Carol stopped herself as tears started running down her face.

"And then what?" I said, encouraging her to finish her sentence.

"And then I am *really* alone. . . . You abandon me, even though you promise not to go off with your brothers and leave me alone with your mom, your sister, or whoever else is giving me the cold shoulder. Heck, you don't even remember what happened. It's like you just want to cross the latest family visit off your to-do list."

Families are one of the main sources of conflict for couples, and conflicts over family can even lead to divorce. Setting boundaries is one of the best remedies for such conflicts.

"It sounds like you do need to take a sabbatical from them until the situation changes," I said. "The question for both of you is, is what you're doing—Carol bending over backward to please them, and Bob just going along with whatever the family wants—making things better or worse? Not just in your marriage, but with your family as well. Are you happy? Is *anyone* happy?"

Neither one of them responded.

I went on. "Bob, what Carol is saying is that when you don't say no to your family, you are saying no to the relationship . . . to your wife."

Both their faces softened. Carol and Bob were looking at each other now, and I could see that the anger and the blame had started to melt away. In Bob's case, they were replaced by empathy for the little girl inside Carol who needed to be seen, appreciated, and accepted as a *person*. Again, they weren't really fighting about what they were fighting about. Carol needed to be heard and understood, and to know she was number one.

"Listen," Carol said. "I need to know that *we* are the family—you and me. I need to know that I come first."

"You do come first," Bob said. "How can I make you believe that?"

"Actions speak louder than words," she said.

"I . . . I guess I could text my sister back and suggest some hotels in the area," Bob said. "I'll do that. I *want* to do that."

He took thirty seconds and typed a quick response. It wasn't another thirty seconds before his BlackBerry beeped with a text from his sister, which he read out loud. "She said, 'I want my brother back.'" He looked at Carol and smiled knowingly. "Wow . . . I think I have a little work to do on why I am so afraid to say no to them. I think I'm starting to get it," said Bob. At least for the moment, it took saying no to his sister to say *yes* to his relationship with Carol.

We continued our session, and Carol agreed not to bring up past grievances but to focus on what Bob was starting to do *right*. They certainly still had a long way to go. But remember how they'd come into my office? With Carol in the lead and Bob with his nose stuck in his Black-Berry? They walked out as a couple, hand in hand.

3-MINUTE FIX

♡

HEARD AND UNDERSTOOD

Listen means "to hear with understanding." You listen not just with your ears, but with your heart and your whole being. Listening isn't just hearing the words that fall out of your partner's mouth and parroting those words back; it's giving the other person the sense that you really get it. Really getting it translates into really getting me. When you don't get it, it's the responsibility of your partner to say, "No, you didn't hear me," and to try again. You'll know when you've heard your partner, because you'll be affected by what he or she said. And your partner will know by your body language that you heard. So often it isn't about the words you say in response. Your partner can *feel* when you get what he or she is communicating. Experience with girlfriends and patients has shown me that most women have built-in BS monitors, which alert them when things are off. The words they hear might be accurate, but they can sense when the intention or understanding is not there.

The best way to listen is to break the conversation into small chunks. At first, it can be really hard for the other person to refrain from saying all the things he or she feels the need to say at once, so make sure you both know that you'll get your chance to talk. Give each other five minutes to talk and then reverse roles. Then take each five-minute statement bit by bit, checking in often to make sure your partner is really hearing what you're saying or that your partner feels that he or she is being heard and understood.

Sometimes just this experience of opening your heart to your partner's message can resolve the conflict loop that has kept you trapped for so long. When a couple comes to see me, and one of the partners says, "I don't get it. I have listened and listened and said I am sorry for months, years, but she just won't drop it!" my response is often the same: "You must listen with your heart and your whole being so that your partner feels heard and understood."

THE FIRE-BREATHER AND THE EGGSHELL WALKER

Andy was a charismatic thirty-six-year-old with his own computer consulting business. His wife, Charlotte, was an elementary school teacher before she became a stay-at-home mom to their son and daughter, now seven and eight. They met ten years ago at a mutual friend's wedding. "She was the cute girl at table eight," Andy said with a smile. "I asked her to dance, and I *don't* dance. That's how I knew she was the one."

"And what brings you here today?" I asked after the introductions were over.

Andy's smile disappeared. "Ask her," he said, folding his arms.

After a pause, Charlotte responded, "He's mad all the time."

"*All* the time?" Andy said. "Come on, Char. That's ridiculous."

"Can you give me some examples, Charlotte?" I asked.

"At home, if the kids are making a mess or being loud, even laughing in the background when he's on the phone, he shouts at them. Or he shouts at me for not controlling them," she said. "When we're out together, everything upsets him. Waiting in line, the price of things at the store, slow salespeople, you name it. Sometimes, he's just grouchy, but a lot of times he really yells. And when traffic's bad, like on the way here today? I stay quiet and just pray that we'll get where we're going fast, because it's really unpleasant being in the car with him."

"Andy," I asked, "does that sound pretty accurate?"

Andy shrugged. "I'm not one to hide my feelings. Yeah, I lose my temper. But it's not like I'd ever *hit* anyone. I don't see why it's such a big deal."

"It is to me," Charlotte said, looking down at her hands. "It didn't used to be this bad, or maybe I just got used to walking on eggshells, but now with the kids, when I see them react to you—how scared they get—sometimes I think about leaving."

Andy snapped his head in her direction. "Leaving? As in getting a divorce?"

Charlotte wouldn't look up. "I don't want the kids to live like this. I don't want this to be their childhood."

"Andy," I said, "what's going on inside you right now, as you're hearing that?"

"What do you think?" he snapped, his face turning red. "I can't believe she's talking like this!"

We all get angry at times, such as when our feelings get hurt or our buttons get pushed, when someone cuts us off in traffic or jumps ahead of us in line, or when our expectations aren't met or things just don't go according to plan. Anger is normal and can even be productive: it can wake us up; it can motivate us to make difficult changes. But for some people, like Andy, anger becomes a go-to emotion, a substitute for a range of other uncomfortable feelings. I call people like this "fire-breathers."

As I've said before, anger can be a way not to feel what's beneath, such as shame or vulnerability. Anger can look like it's working, but is it really? If you make your partner shut down, you may get what you want in the short term, but what does it lead to down the line? Anger can also be a toxic way to control others—to get your way and to make people do what you want them to do. That's when a gut check is really important. Do you really want to control your significant other, or is anger just your habitual reaction? Do you really want a partner who complies out of fear rather than love and respect?

"I don't think he realizes how hard it is for us," Charlotte said. "Or how much tension there is in the house. The minute he comes home from work, we're on high alert. When he leaves the house in the morning, you can practically hear all of us exhale."

I could well believe it. Andy was sitting there with his jaw clenched, tense from the effort of letting, at my request, Charlotte speak without interruption. The fact that he could show some restraint, however, was encouraging.

"Do you have a sense of how your anger could be purposeful?" I asked him.

"What do you mean?" he said. "Something happens. I get angry. I react."

"Were you like this as a little kid?"

He actually snorted. "Are you kidding? Not in *my* house."

"Where did you grow up?"

Andy relaxed a little bit. "Indiana. Small town."

"Big family?"

"Four boys." His face softened. "My mom was like Betty Crocker, always cooking. She was great . . . and my dad ran a pretty tight ship."

"He was the disciplinarian?"

"Oh yeah."

Andy went on to explain that in *his* house, there had been little room for mistakes. Punishment had been quick and severe. He remembered his dad being angry all the time.

"Don't get me wrong," Andy said. "He loved us. You just never wanted him mad at you, that's for damn sure."

"It sounds scary," I said. "Like . . . you were walking on eggshells?"

Andy stared at me for a moment, then turned to Charlotte, with a rueful look. "Wow. I guess I have turned into my dad."

This was a powerful insight for Andy. Although he loved his father and had grown close to him as an adult, Andy's childhood memories were a mixed bag, and not a legacy he wanted to pass on to his own children. But anger is a tough habit to break. It's almost like an addiction, as the fire-breather learns to depend on intimidation. Anger can give the fire-breather a temporary sense of power and control; it can make him or her feel invincible in the moment . . . but as with substance abuse, when the high is gone, the pain and destruction that the fire-breather was attempting to flee are right there waiting.

This is the Blame Game and the Shame Spiral. Andy was invoking his childhood rage and looking for a target. If your partner responds in kind, you're off to the races. And if your partner acts like Charlotte—shushing the kids, apologizing to the waiter, working hard to anticipate or avoid anything that will set you off, and doing damage control when those efforts fail—the result is hardly any better. This is exhausting for all parties involved. And what is the effect on the underlying problem? You guessed it: Bubkis. Nothing at all.

So, how do you turn it around?

I asked Andy to close his eyes and share with us a memory from his childhood.

"My mom has this photo of me in kindergarten," he said, "where I look exactly like our son. To this day, it's hanging in her den. I was the scrawniest kid in school, and I think I cried every day until fourth grade." He smiled. "Mom said she was worried I'd be crying all the way to college."

"Did something change in fourth grade?" I asked.

He hesitated, then cleared his throat. "I got beat up on the playground for crying, and I learned to toughen up. Hit back harder."

It wasn't hard for Andy to see that he'd replaced the emotions of fear and sorrow with his dad's brand of explosiveness. This, he realized, had become standard operating procedure, not just for him, but for his brothers, as well.

I explained to Charlotte that she was going to have to work on saying over and over to Andy, "Listen, if you want to talk about what you're feeling, I'm available. If you continue to rage, I'm not. I'm taking the kids and going to the movies or on a walk or to the library. I am not going to walk on eggshells or allow the kids to be in the middle of this." And then the next step for anyone in this situation, as challenging as it may be, is to literally walk the walk. If you say you are leaving, you have to follow through.

Charlotte dug deeper and acknowledged that another reason why she wanted to take care of this now was that it was bringing up memories of her efforts to keep the peace between her own parents. "I am done stuffing down my feelings with food, like I did as a kid. I see our girls doing the same thing when *we* fight—Abby standing in front of the refrigerator, grazing, and Jennifer trying keep us from fighting."

If find yourself walking on eggshells when your partner vents their anger, the loving thing to do for yourself and your partner is to find the emotional courage to set boundaries and then to follow through with them. It may be hard for you to forgive your partner for his or her anger. But what about feeling compassion for the child who was forced to learn how to use anger in this way? Digging back to the origins of the anger, how it served us or was modeled for us when we were children, can help us not only understand our behaviors, but also, more importantly, view ourselves and our partners with compassion, curiosity, and patience. This doesn't mean that you should tolerate your partner's anger or even be available to take it. That is not being loving to your partner or to yourself. The partner who is angry needs to do the work to manage his or her anger and also needs to take full responsibility for it and what lies beneath.

More often than not these anger and shame cycles are passed down from generation to generation. You can make the commitment to yourself and to your family that it stops with you. You can heal your own wounds by being the parent (to your own children) that you wish you had had, by using the family of your childhood or your "offending" parent as a model for what you *do not* want to be as an adult. Often, parents don't realize the profound impact that growing up in the cross fire of verbal and/or physical abuse has on children. Although the vitriolic words and actions may not be directed at them, the experience can actually do more damage than if they were the target of the rage.

The process of change began for Andy that day in my office, but I knew that he'd have to do the real work of replacing anger with loving behavior at home, at the office, in commuter traffic, and elsewhere. I taught him techniques to overcome his anger (we'll get into those later in this chapter), but I knew the process would be slow, sometimes tedious, and often frustrating. However, I could see that Andy had the *intention* to change and that recognizing the effect his anger had on his children was a strong motivator. As long as Andy could hold on to his commitment, and Charlotte could support him by not acquiescing to his anger and by taking care of herself, he had a good chance of stopping the anger and not passing this behavior, inherited from his father, on to his children. He could learn for himself, and simultaneously teach his children, how to deal with conflict in a healthy and productive way.

Charlotte had the opportunity to break the multigenerational pattern she had inherited and to be a strong and healthy role model for her daughters. Instead of unwittingly encouraging them to walk on eggshells, as her own mother had encouraged her to do, and passing on the erroneous belief that this was the way to keep the peace, Charlotte needed to model setting boundaries for how others treat her and then follow through in enforcing them. In other words, knowing your self-worth and being loving to yourself and your partner.

We need a reality check: we're a culture of enablers. Acquiescing to a partner's anger is like giving your kids a bunch of cookies every time they cry. Be honest with yourself. Sticking your head in the sand may be the quickest way to make your partner's anger go away, but is it a loving action toward yourself? The obvious alternative isn't so hot, either: meeting your partner's anger with your own just makes an explosive situation worse. In this situation, loving behavior takes extreme emotional courage. (If you feel as if it also takes *physical courage,* then please, please seek the help and support of a licensed mental health provider.)

Remember, the loving thing for both you and your partner to do is to refuse to accept this anger—to set boundaries on the anger that your partner is allowed to dump on you and to find healthy ways to respond and to take care of yourself. Perhaps you must do as Charlotte, who is going to have to work on saying over and over, "Listen, if you want to talk about what you're feeling, I'm available. But if you continue to rage, I'm not." Remember, what's loving for yourself, what supports your own emotional or spiritual growth in the *long run,* is also loving for the other person. And if you have kids in the equation, it's important to keep in mind what's loving for *them* and what you are modeling.

PROCESSING ANGER

Just as we learn how to express love by following our parents' example, we learn how to process anger by modeling (or rebelling against) our parents' behaviors. Some of us are "taught," either explicitly or implicitly, to yell when we get upset; and some of us are taught to repress our anger.

If you're the eggshell walker . . .

If you are the target of a loved one's anger, use this exercise to mitigate feelings of powerlessness and to avoid engaging with your partner's rage. By exploring your part in the conflict and by brainstorming healthier, more loving choices, you can find healthy ways to take care of yourself. Answer the following questions to help you get started.

When my partner gets angry, my normal reaction is to . . .

_____

_____

Your answers might include the following: Try to calm him or her down. Get angry back and try to convince my partner that he or she is

wrong. Give in, give up, and hit the emergency stash of cupcakes in the
pantry for times like this. Go on Facebook and see what my ex is up to.

What happens as a result?

_____

_____

Does the conflict loop grow stronger, or is the situation diffused?

_____

_____

Perhaps you know that your reaction isn't helping, and you're ready to explore some healthier choices. What would some loving actions be? Create a list of these, which you can return to in the heat of the moment.

_____

_____

_____

Your answers might include the following: Going for a walk. Losing myself in a good book. Patting myself on the back for walking away and not engaging. Writing about my feelings in a journal. Calling a trusted friend. Meditating. Spending time in nature.

Tune in to what it's like to be on the receiving end of your partner's anger. How does it make you feel?

_____

_____

Your answers might include the following: Scared. Angry. Hopeless.

Can you remember an earlier time in your life, before you met your partner, when something or someone evoked the same feelings in you?

_____

_____

What physical reactions do you have when faced with your partner's anger?

_____

_____

Your answers might include the following: My heart races. My shoulders shrug up by my ears or get tense. My breathing becomes shallow. I get nauseated.

Do you remember a time when someone other than your partner was really, really angry with you? When did this happen, and who got angry?

_____

What is something nurturing you can do for yourself right now?

_____

_____

The next time your partner is breathing fire, let it be known that as long as he or she is raging, you are not available. Say, "When you want to talk and really explore what is going on and resolve the conflict, I am available." Walk away, hang up the phone, stop texting, and do something nurturing for yourself. Return to your list of loving actions if you need some inspiration.

If you're the fire-breather . . .

When you are able to recognize that your anger is building, you can make the choice to do something about it before it becomes unmanageable. This is where the practice of mindfulness is invaluable. You can take control of the situation before you do or say something that you will regret. If you are a fire-breather and have trouble managing your anger, take some time to explore and understand the fear, pain, or shame that may be lurking underneath the anger.

What are your body's signals that tell you your anger is escalating?

_____

_____

Your answers might include the following: My heart races. My jaw clenches. My voice gets loud.

Where does this anger come from? Is it a learned behavior? If so, from whom did you learn this behavior? What happened when that person or those people got angry? This can be a tough question to answer at first, and you may draw a blank, but "I don't know" won't get you anywhere!

_____

_____

Your answers might include the following: Yes, it's a learned behavior. I learned it from Dad or Mom. His/her anger got me/us to shut up. It became an excuse to bail, or it justified another bad behavior, such as drinking, spending too much money, or sneaking around.

Can you recall a time when someone's anger really scared you?

_____

_____

Has your partner ever told you that your anger scares him or her? If so, how did that make you feel?

_____

_____

With your partner, do you use anger to get your way? When? In these situations, what do you really want from your partner? Is it compliance or fear or subservience? Now think about what you want in the long run. Is it love or peace?

_____

_____

How do you feel about your anger, not the rush of adrenaline and the sense of power it gives you in the moment, but later, after the anger has died down? Do you feel good, bad, guilty, sad?

_____

_____

Think about the ways in which your anger affords you protection. If you couldn't feel angry, how would you feel instead? Vulnerable? Out of control? Powerless? Weak?

_____

_____

What are some ways in which you can take a time-out when you feel your anger rising? List some options here. You can refer back to this list in the heat of the moment.

_____

_____

_____

Your answers might include the following: Go for a run, a walk, or a swim. Clean up the backyard. Meditate. Call a friend (one who *will be honest and who has my best interests in mind). Write in my journal. Turn to a HEARTwork exercise I can do on my own. Go to an anger management meeting or call my sponsor (if applicable).*

It is best not to wait until you are on the verge of an angry outburst to figure out the most effective ways to manage your emotions. Often our physiology takes over in these situations, and it can be challenging to think clearly. Rehearse in advance what you are going to do in the event that you feel your anger rising. Consult the list of time-outs you created to self-regulate your temper.

NO TRUST = NO RELATIONSHIP

Molly, forty-four, was a news anchor for a major television network, and even in her off-camera clothes—jeans, cashmere sweater, loafers—she turned heads. Her husband, Julian, looked more like a surfer, which he was, with his sun-streaked hair and appealing, crinkly smile. Julian was an executive at an HR firm.

"You sounded really upset on the phone," I said to Molly as she took a seat in my office.

"Yeah," said Molly. "I found out last week he's having an affair. I'm so . . . embarrassed."

"I keep telling her I'm sorry!" said Julian. "How many times can I apologize? I don't know how many times I can say it."

"How did you find out?" I asked Molly.

"For a long time I had this gut feeling. I hate women

who are always snooping, but then, last week, I looked at his phone, and there were texts from another woman."

"Did this come as a surprise to you?" I asked.

"Yes and no," she said. "Yes, because this is something I would never expect him to do. And no, because for a really long time something didn't feel right in my gut. And I would say to him, 'It just seems like all these business trips, and you couldn't call me because you were drunk or whatever. . . .' It just didn't seem right. And he would say, 'You're jealous or paranoid or possessive.'"

"So you were being gaslighted?" I asked.

The term *gaslight* comes from the 1938 play *Gas Light,* in which a husband tries to convince his wife that she's insane in order to institutionalize her and steal her inheritance. One of the ways he does this is by dimming the house's gaslights and then, when his wife notices, insisting that she's imaging things. *Gaslighting* has become a psychological term in our culture that describes a situation in which the person doing the gaslighting deflects their partner's suspicion or sidesteps questions by attacking their perception of reality. Over time, the person being gaslighted goes against what their gut is telling them: *Maybe my partner* is *telling the truth.* The most devastating part of gaslighting is that after drinking your lying partner's Kool-Aid, eventually you stop trusting yourself. And it doesn't take Charles Boyer futzing with a gas meter (in the 1944 film adaptation of the play); it's actually more common than you may think.

I can't believe you would accuse me of that. That says more
    about you than it says about me.
What do you mean, I'm acting weird? You're acting weird.
I never said that. You're making things up.
You're just being jealous. You always blow things out of
    proportion.
These shoes? I've had them forever!
You never told me that I had to pick up the kids after school.
I know I reminded you I was going out with my girlfriends.

These are all examples of verbal gaslighting—
manipulating another person's perception of reality by
deflecting suspicion, sidestepping questions, lying, and
denying wrongdoing. I see it when one partner in a couple
is drinking, and I see it with cheating. And this tactic
can work. Molly, for instance, was in danger of losing her
healthy instincts and even her sanity. Over time, she started
to doubt herself, even though her suspicions continued
to eat away at her. She wanted to believe Julian's explanations, and so she put her own good judgment on the back
burner.

"All right! I'm sorry. It's awful. It was a bad mistake.
But she's been preoccupied with work and the kids and all
of that, and I was just feeling left out," Julian said.

I was starting to understand why Molly wouldn't accept
his apology. But then Molly started apologizing herself.

"I know, I just . . . With my career, it's really hard to
keep everything going," she said. "I know I haven't been as
available as I could be."

Julian was nodding.

"Look, Molly," I said gently, "you know, it's really hard to hear you accepting this blame."

"Well, I feel bad," Julian began. "But . . ." He trailed off, not following up with anything that showed that he got it.

We've seen a lot of guilt in this book—guilt about what you wish you had or had not done in the past, guilt over not being the person you wish you were now. But there's another kind of guilt. Actually, that guilt is shame, and it's *healthy shame.* Healthy shame is the feeling you have when you genuinely know that what you did was wrong, that you acted in a way that is toxic to your relationship and your sense of self. Healthy shame serves a good purpose: it's a corrective emotional experience. It becomes an opportunity to learn from this egregious behavior and contributes to your partner's piece of mind that it won't happen again. Healthy shame is a normal and very human emotion. The first step in the challenge of overcoming an affair and rebuilding a marriage is for the person who cheated to feel *authentic, healthy shame* . . . and I just wasn't seeing that from Julian.

So I was concerned, but not all that surprised, when Molly canceled our second session. Over the phone, she explained that everything was fine, that she'd been overreacting.

Two months later, she and Julian were back in my office.

"You know what?" Molly said as soon as she sat down. "I stopped shaming myself for being suspicious, and I checked his phone records, Facebook, all that. And this wasn't just a one-time thing. I don't believe it's even ended!"

There it was. This whole time I'd been wondering where her anger was.

"Is she prettier than me? Sexier than me?" Molly yelled at Julian. "You know what? You're saying the words, but I really don't think you're getting my pain. Not only was this devastating, but now I'm finding out these women you cheated with watch me on TV. God, they know who I am! I just feel so exposed, so violated! Were they at the station fund-raiser? Did you invite them to the holiday party at our house?"

"Okay, I really do feel badly. I'm such a creep. You are the last person who should feel shame. I really get it. Shame on me. *You* have nothing to feel embarrassed about," Julian said.

I was beginning to believe him this time. Still, this couple had a rough road ahead.

Couples *can* survive an affair, but there are four nonnegotiable conditions the two partners must meet to get past the infidelity:

1. Both partners must be committed to saving the relationship.
2. The person who did the cheating must authentically feel *healthy shame*—the kind of shame that becomes a corrective mechanism.
3. All communication with the "other" man or woman must end.
4. The person who did the cheating must allow his or her partner to express anger freely—and not just once.

The third condition requires *total transparency*. I told

Julian, "I want you to invite Molly to check your e-mail, everything, as much as she wants to. Give her all your passwords. And you need to come totally clean about things she wants to know about the past. She's going to need to fill in those holes."

Earlier in this chapter I described expressing anger as "dumping it" on our partner—and that's generally not a good thing. But in the case of an affair, it is essential to give the person who has been betrayed the opportunity to express outrage about the infidelity. In other words, raw anger is an essential step for moving forward. Once Julian agreed to absolute transparency in his social exchanges so that Molly could know for sure that all communication between him and the other woman had stopped, it was time for Molly to move on to the fourth nonnegotiable condition: freely expressing her anger.

"I don't know how many times or how many ways I can say I'm sorry," Julian said. "It just doesn't seem to help."

"Julian," I asked, "are you ready to really *hear* Molly?"

Julian leaned forward, elbows on his knees. "I hear that she's mad. I've been hearing it for the past month, since the night she found out."

"You think it's just going to disappear?" Molly asked incredulously. "Just because you're sorry? After all the lies you told me?"

I intervened gently as Julian geared up to respond. "Julian, are you willing to just sit and hear, with no explanations or self-defense? To just stay present and let Molly tell you everything she's feeling?"

"Okay, but how about what I'm feeling?" he replied.

I shook my head. "It's not about you right now."

Julian ran a hand through his hair, took a deep breath, and nodded. It was encouraging to see Julian move closer to his wife and become focused and present with her in a way I hadn't seen before.

For several minutes Molly let out her feelings of rage, heartache, and betrayal. She gave voice to her fears about being left for another woman, to the nightmare of doubting her own instincts and even her common sense, and to her embarrassment.

"I turn to you and see this man I loved, and I don't know who you are. And I don't even know who I am anymore. I'm so ashamed that I didn't see this, didn't trust myself . . . I am so ashamed." As this last word came out of her, her anger subsided, and she seemed to shrink into the corner of the sofa.

"Ashamed of what?" I asked.

Molly only shook her head, unable to look at either Julian or me.

"Is this feeling, this shame . . . *familiar*?" I asked.

After a sudden intake of breath, Molly went still. I waited.

Julian looked at her, then back at me. "I'm not sure what's going on right now."

"Why don't you ask her?" I said. "Ask her from a place of real curiosity."

"Molly?" he said gently. "Could you tell me what's going on?"

In a small voice, she said, "I'm thinking about my mom."

"What about her?" Julian asked, clearly confused. "You

know," he added, "if it's all right for me to say this, when I ask you about your childhood, you get quiet."

Molly wrapped her arms around herself protectively. "Okay, you know she's sober. She got sober when I was in college. But all through my growing-up years, when we were walking home from school, we never knew, my brother and me, who'd be in the house, waiting for us. Dr. Jekyll or Mrs. Hyde."

"Where was your dad in all this?" I asked.

"He was a surgeon. He worked really long hours. It was hard for him."

"And for you," I said gently.

Molly nodded. "I never had friends over. I didn't do sports or after-school activities, because I didn't want to leave my little brother alone with Mom."

"Was she abusive?" I asked.

Molly's face crumpled. "Not when she was sober."

It's an old story. As they grow up, children who are abused or who have alcoholic parents or parents with a substance abuse, an eating disorder, or a history of infidelity— anything than engenders shame and secrecy—learn to abide by the spoken or unspoken family rules about keeping the family's secrets. They learn to pretend that things are "normal" and to cover for others' behaviors. They are often afraid to bring their friends home, lest their friends discover the family's secrets. This secrecy, this strict adherence to "Don't ask, don't tell," creates a sense of shame in children, and that shame, once internalized, travels with the children into adulthood. The fact that the children did nothing wrong in no way diminishes these feelings of shame, and this shame erodes their sense of self.

The shame they bear is really toxic shame. *Healthy shame,* that is, the feeling that arises when we acknowledge having wronged someone or having done wrong, is both normal and essential. It comes with having a conscience. *Toxic shame,* however, is the pervasive feeling that who we are, rather than what we have done, is condemnable, and therefore we are unworthy, unlovable, and defective. Toxic shame sufferers have taken on the shame that rightfully belongs to another. People who suffer from toxic shame experience some degree of self-loathing, which in turn makes it difficult for them to reveal, even to their partner, their authentic self. Thus having and sustaining intimate relationships can be really challenging for them.

Toxic shame needn't come from something as clear-cut as having an alcoholic parent. There are many other family secrets, such as those related to poverty, depression, a particular religious affiliation, or even a particular ethnicity—anything that would make you feel like you had to hide this aspect of yourself from the world, lest you be judged or rejected. And what's so important is being able to see that you aren't responsible for these things. This toxic shame doesn't rightfully belong to you. This shame belongs to the abusive parent or to the kids at school who bullied you for not being dressed the right way.

If you can get in touch with those times when you felt toxic shame—when you didn't want to be "found out," as if there was an unspoken rule to keep a secret—then you can work to let go of this shame, which doesn't belong to you.

In many ways, Molly had become "shame based." Molly's shame stemming from Julian's affair didn't really belong to her—it belonged to Julian. But because she had learned to internalize the toxic shame of her mother's drinking while she was young, it was pretty darn easy for Molly to take on Julian's shame now.

"I always felt there was something," Julian said. "This is a big part of you that I didn't know about. Not that an affair needed to happen for this, but right now I am really getting it. I have exposed you in that way again and have allowed you to experience humiliation because of something I did. . . . I really, really do feel ashamed."

As he watched Molly huddle miserably in her corner of the sofa, arms hugging her knees, Julian's own distress was evident. Molly was a world away from him, and he feared that she wasn't going to let him back in.

"I wonder—even before you suspected the affair, have you ever felt that you were keeping your head in the sand about the problems you had been having?" I asked, handing Molly the tissue box.

Molly blew her nose. "Maybe. The truth is, our marriage has been off course for a while."

"Have you felt it, too?" I asked, turning to Julian.

He nodded. "We've talked about coming to therapy for a long time now, but we always had a reason for putting it off." Tentatively, Julian moved closer to Molly and reached for her hand.

Now we were ready to do the work. It wasn't that Molly and Julian were somehow magically "beyond" the affair, but they were ready to start slowly building trust back into the relationship, while looking at how they could make it better so that something like this never happened again. The repair didn't happen overnight; it took a long time to set this relationship on the road to recovery. We met for more than a year, and it was hard work.

Finally, after more than a year had elapsed, during which Julian remained true to his word and observed total transparency, with no slipping, Molly was ready to try to forgive and let go. This is an important step; otherwise, if the other person feels like there's no chance of ever being forgiven, why try? Moving forward didn't mean that trust issues would never come up again in their relationship. But once Julian expressed *authentic, healthy shame* for his behavior, showed a willingness to provide *total transparency* for Molly, and let her *express her anger,* sadness, fear, and pain, Molly was willing to open her heart to Julian again and take a risk.

TOTAL TRANSPARENCY

Let's address the obvious right now: there is no 3-Minute Fix for infidelity. Ripping down trust may take only a few minutes, but it takes a long time to rebuild it. We talked about transparency in this chapter, but let's go a bit deeper into what it *really* means. Exhibiting total transparency in an effort to rebuild trust in a relationship means that if you say you'll be home at 7:30 P.M., you're home at 7:30 P.M. "What if there's a traffic jam?" you ask? It used to be no big deal if you came home late because of traffic. Those days are over, my friend. If there's a traffic jam, you call your partner and you stay on the phone as you drive home. If you don't, you open a Pandora's box of other possibilities. Are you lying? Are you not lying? Your partner can't be sure.

But here's the thing, even if you act in a trustworthy way, your partner is still going to have a hard time trusting you because of the time(s) you betrayed that trust. Which means now is the time for going overboard, for being 100 percent committed to trust building. Not one step out of line, for it could truly mean the end of the relationship this time.

You may even consider making little agreements with your partner just so that you can keep them and show that you're trustworthy. For example, agree that you will be home by a set time (on the dot), and if something happens to hold you up, like a downed tree on the state highway, make a phone call and tell your partner to turn on the news to verify that a tree, indeed, is blocking traffic on the highway. Or if you're going out to lunch or to a business dinner, you might agree to let your partner know in advance where you're going and who you will be with. If you go to the corner store, tell your partner when you'll be back, and then stick to the schedule. You're past the point of being able to talk with your partner about your trustworthiness—it's going to take total transparency and follow-through, honoring these agreements over and over and over again, in order to rebuild trust.

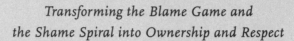

HEARTwork

*Transforming the Blame Game and
the Shame Spiral into Ownership and Respect*

Exercise 1: The Blame Game and the Shame Spiral Quiz

Find out if you and your partner are stuck in the Blame Game and the Shame Spiral conflict loop. Read the following statements, and for each one, circle the number for the response that comes closest to how you feel.

---
1 = Strongly Disagree, 2 = Disagree, 3 = Agree, 4 = Strongly Agree

---

1. My partner never takes any responsibility for his or her part in our conflicts.

                                     1   2   3   4

2. My partner uses blame or anger to get his or her way.

       1   2   3   4

3. My partner's anger scares me.

       1   2   3   4

4. If I keep my mouth shut, I can prevent conflict.

       1   2   3   4

5. After one of our fights I squelch my feelings with food or sneak a cigarette or do something else that feels good to me that I know my partner would disapprove of.

       1   2   3   4

6. I often feel like one of us is walking on eggshells.

       1   2   3   4

7. We seem to spend all our time fighting about who is right and who is wrong.

	1	2	3	4

8. We can't even talk about an issue that needs to be resolved without getting into a yelling match.

	1	2	3	4

9. When we're done fighting, I'm ashamed of what I said to my partner.

	1	2	3	4

10. There is so much anger in our relationship that I never feel turned on.

	1	2	3	4

11. I'm afraid that without my anger, I would be too vulnerable.

	1	2	3	4

12. Growing up, I believed I could control my parents' anger by getting angry myself or walking on eggshells or being the peacemaker between them.

	1	2	3	4

13. I can remember times as I was growing up when I felt profound shame.

	1	2	3	4

14. I wish my partner would just shut up for a second so that he or she could hear what I'm saying.

	1	2	3	4

15. Sometimes when we fight, I feel like I'm going crazy.

	1	2	3	4

16. The truth has gotten so twisted around, I'm not even sure what's real anymore.

	1	2	3	4

17. My partner sees his or her point of view as more valid or "real" than mine.

| 1 | 2 | 3 | 4 |

18. If I am angry long enough or patient enough about my partner's anger, eventually it will go away.

| 1 | 2 | 3 | 4 |

19. I have crazy revenge fantasies, like cleaning my partner's toilet bowl with his or her toothbrush.

| 1 | 2 | 3 | 4 |

20. I am ashamed of who I have become or who my partner has become.

| 1 | 2 | 3 | 4 |

Scoring: Add up the numbers you circled for your total score.

Below 35: If your score is below 35, you aren't trapped in the Blame Game and the Shame Spiral conflict loop, but it might still be worthwhile to give some thought to the statements for which you circled a 4. Consider talking to your partner about these, too. Talking about these issues now could prevent this conflict loop from forming or could help you disentangle yourself from one of the other conflict loops described in this book.

35–50: Blame, shame, and anger are definitely issues in your relationship. Complete the following HEARTwork exercises to help you start diffusing the conflict.

51 or above: Because the Blame Game and the Shame Spiral is such a volatile conflict loop, in addition to completing the following HEARTwork exercises, you might want to seek professional help to work safely through this conflict.

Exercise 2: Release Anger (Without Dumping It on Your Partner)

If you're feeling shut down and angry, this two-step exercise will help you release your anger and access your more loving feelings in a healthy and intentional way.

Sometimes you have no choice but to vent your anger, but dumping it on your partner is usually not the most productive way to do it. Here's a healthy alternative. Instead of dumping your anger on your partner, dump it on a piece of paper and compose what I call an Angry Purge Letter.

As you write your letter, give yourself permission to get angry. Play the victim. Blame and shame all you want. Be as critical toward your partner as you need to be. For example, allow yourself to write, "I'm miserable, and my life is awful because of you! How did I ever end up married to someone like you? All I ever feel is disappointment, loneliness, and sadness, and it's all your fault."

Write down all your emotions until you feel dried up and the feelings beneath the anger start coming up—sadness, longing, whatever they are. Then *no being sneaky!* No "accidentally" leaving your letter around where your partner might find it and read it. Tear it up or burn it.

With the anger gone and your more vulnerable feelings out in the open, now you are ready for some heartfelt face-to-face intimacy with your partner. Now is the time to share what you feel sad or scared about or responsible for:

I feel sad and lonely when we fight.
I feel badly about myself when I blame you; and I get angry, when what I really want is to love you.
I feel sad that I punish, hurt, or push you away with my anger.

I feel scared when you say this is not the life you want or maybe our relationship is a mistake.

Next, share your hopes and dreams and love:

I wish we could find our way back to the love we once had.
I want us to grow old together.
I love and admire that you never give up on us.

With the anger gone and your heart open, you now have a reality check, as well as an idea of the payoff that awaits you once you do this HEARTwork and access the good feelings that are there. This is a productive exercise, even if your partner is currently unavailable to take part in it.

Exercise 3: Managing Your Body's Response to Anger

If your challenge has been to disable your automatic reaction of anger or shame, here's another tool to help you stick with your intention. We've talked about mindfulness before—about the precious moment between what happens (the trigger) and how you react, that tiny window of opportunity in which taking a mindful breath can help undermine an automatic reaction and allow you to stop and choose a loving response. Being mindful about taking a breath before reacting negatively is a way to diffuse not only anger that "starts" with you, but also "hot" anger, or the fury aroused in you by your partner's anger. This HEARTwork exercise will hone your mindful breathing skills. It is about bringing yourself back to the present moment, which is a challenge for all of us.

Start by devoting five minutes to this exercise (though twenty would be great). Here's what to do: Take a seat and assume a comfortable position, place your hands on the tops of your thighs or over your heart, close your eyes, and breathe. Notice the air filling and escaping your lungs, your belly rising and falling; concentrate on the sound of each and every breath. If your focus occasionally wanders—if you realize that you're suddenly thinking about what to have for lunch or what's left on today's to-do list—that's okay. Simply acknowledge the thought, and then return your focus to your breathing. Now, as you breathe in for four counts, say a positive word or a short phrase, such as "Peace" or "All is well," and think about breathing in love and peace, and taking a cleansing breath. As you breathe out for six counts, visualize exhaling any tension or stress. Keep it simple.

This mindful breathing exercise, this meditation, is another positive activity that the two of you can do together, as it benefits both the individual and the couple, creating a general sense of peace in the home. There is a beautiful energy that happens when you meditate together. Over time, this exercise might become a wonderful ritual to do together, one that deepens not only your connection to yourself but also to each other.

How to Survive an Affair

In chapter 5 we saw a couple face infidelity and work to rebuild a loving, trusting relationship. In order to get past the infidelity, they had to meet several nonnegotiable conditions and take some important steps. This exercise is a review of that process.

Both partners must be committed to saving the relationship. And after an affair, that's not a given. Be honest with yourself about whether you *want* to save the relationship. Only if the answer is yes for both of you, move on to evaluating and addressing the other conditions.

The partner who cheated must feel *authentic, healthy* shame. The only way to move forward with the next steps is if the cheating partner feels truly ashamed in his or her heart and soul about the behavior. Authentic shame is a corrective emotion: it alerts us to the "dangers" of our behavior and keeps us from repeating bad behaviors. It is the feeling that comes when we acknowledge having wronged someone or having done wrong, and it is not just normal but also essential and makes us human. It comes with having a conscience.

All communication with the "other" man or woman must end. This may seem like a given, but I can't emphasize enough how important it is for the partner who has cheated to end the affair—completely. That means no e-mails, no phone calls, no texting, and no "friendly lunches" (that's likely how the person who cheated got into this mess). Both partners should discuss exactly how to do this, and the cheating partner must be willing to practice total transparency. If the partner who has been cheated on wants to listen in on the "breakup" phone call or read the Dear John or Dear Jane letter, he or she should be allowed to do so. And the cheating partner can't just say that all communication has ended— he or she has to prove it. This includes freely offering his or her partner all Internet passwords, outing all those "work" cell phones, and opening up about all travel plans and other plans that don't involve his or her partner. The partner who cheated can't ask for trust. Now it's time to "show, not tell."

The person who did the cheating must allow his or her partner to express anger freely—and not just once. Sure, partners in a garden-variety argument make things worse by dumping anger on each other. But this is different. The one who has been cheated on must get it all out.

Partners must be willing to forgive. Once both partners have met the nonnegotiable conditions, the wayward partner has done the work, and enough time has passed to rebuild trust, the partner who was cheated on has to take a leap of faith and offer forgiveness. Without it, the cheater may begin to feel there is no hope for rebuilding the relationship and may simply give up.

True, this step involves being vulnerable and being willing to take a risk. Be kind to yourself. Offering forgiveness is difficult. It may be one of the toughest things you ever do. It is a complex and challenging step, but it's also necessary. Let go of the false assumption that by forgiving, you're dismissing the pain you felt. Let go of the belief that if you forgive your partner, you're condoning the behavior. I know it is tough, and it is very normal and human to feel that way. You may never forget. The memories may never fade entirely. But at some point the partner who was cheated on will have to say, "Enough," and will have to return to the relationship with an open heart.

Honestly and truly, it is possible to survive the crushing heartache and the struggle, and make it to the other side of an affair with a strengthened bond and a newfound loving partnership. Both my own heart and my experience of working with many couples have shown me this.

Chapter 6

• • • • • • •

Testing, Testing, 1, 2, 3 ∞
Profound Trust

I F YOU HAVE children, you probably are smiling to yourself and saying, "I know exactly what testing is. My kids
put me through it every day." It may be easy to recognize
testing in your kids, but sometimes it's hard to acknowledge that we adults test in many ways, too. When we test
our partners, we might be wondering, *Do you love me? Am
I important to you? Will you stay with me? Do I turn you
on? Do I still turn you on? How far can I push things with
money or sexual issues or commitments? Can I exchange just
an e-mail or a text here or there with the ex? That's not so bad,
is it?*

And often, just like children, we may keep testing at
the cost not just of our relationship but also of our own
peace of mind. If you're testing, you're not addressing the
real relationship issues, and you're probably living your

life with low-grade anxiety humming in the background. That's because testing is a pass/fail kind of thing: Will your partner stick around or won't he or she? Can your partner accept you for who you are? And with this testing, you're always worried somewhere in the back of your brain that the answer might be no.

But by testing, what you or your partner is really asking is, "How much do you love me?" The goal of testing isn't to get left (okay, maybe *sometimes* it is). Usually, the goal is to find love or prove love or solidify love—or to guard against disappointment and broken expectations. And, unfortunately, getting yourself stuck in the Testing, Testing, 1, 2, 3 conflict loop is a good way to create the very thing you think you're guarding against. You worry that he or she is going to leave you, and so you test, and by testing you ensure that he or she leaves you. Even if your partner didn't have any intention of leaving you, you'll end up pushing him or her away.

TO COMMIT OR NOT TO COMMIT

"I'm not really sure, but I know I'm feeling a little anxious," Natalie admitted. She looked over at her boyfriend, Owen. "He made the phone call. . . . I'm not really sure why. Maybe he wants to break up with me. . . ."

"Why would you think that?" I asked.

"Because . . . we're not moving forward," said Natalie.

"One of the things I love or loved about her is that she was always really down to earth," Owen said. "And now she just all of a sudden dresses a little more provocatively. It's just not characteristic of her—she's been texting old boyfriends, too. You know, I gotta admit, I'm starting to have my doubts."

"How long have you been dating?" I said.

Natalie and Owen answered in unison.

"Forever," she said.

"Not that long," he said.

Natalie let out a nervous laugh. "Just shy of two years," she said, correcting herself. "We practically live together. I mean, I've held on to my place, but we're together almost every single night."

We've seen a couple of ways that most men are different than most women (though individuals of both genders do break the mold), and here's another one: men and women have very different agendas when it comes to commitment. Women have biological clocks, and men really don't. I'm not saying that every commitment issue can be explained by a woman's body—but it is a reality that women wrestle with their biological clock. Without coming out and saying it, Natalie was asking, "Is this ever going to happen?" and she was thinking to herself, *Now or never!* Owen, on the other hand, felt as if he was in that dream in which you're in class and the test is today and you haven't studied . . . and you're in your underwear. In other words, he felt panicky and unprepared.

There are lots of ways to "test" a partner or a spouse—drinking too much or staying out too late, becoming less available, "flirting" or crossing a line when it comes to someone other than your partner. Deep down, people who constantly test the boundaries with their partners are usually asking, "How far can I push you before you'll leave me? Do you *really* love me? Will you stay with me no matter what?" They're asking if there is something they can do, no matter what it is, to get what they want. In Natalie's case, the desired outcome was a commitment.

Then, you know what? She came out and said it. "Well, I've tried everything to get you to move forward, get engaged, and I'm just starting to wonder if maybe it's me. Maybe I'm not attractive anymore. Maybe I'm not *sexy* anymore, at least not to you. When I wear nice clothes, guys notice me . . . and it feels *good*. And maybe it feels good because I want you to *see* that other guys notice me."

"I know, I know," said Owen. But he wasn't the carefree, afraid-to-commit man he seemed to be, either. It turned out that this wasn't Owen's first rodeo. A forty-year-old and Natalie's elder by six years, he had been engaged twice before. "The first time, I just knew it wasn't right, and I really hurt her," Owen said. "The second time, we'd been living together, and it just seemed like the right thing to do. Then, before the wedding, I guess we just both realized it wasn't right. And now, with Natalie, I think I have been honestly waiting. But you know what?" He turned to Natalie. "I know you really want to get married, Natalie. And you've done a really great job of not pushing, but let me be honest with you. If I had to commit right now, I'd say I need more time. I don't feel the same kind of pressure you do. And just so you know, it doesn't mean I don't love you. I do. I don't look around."

In some ways, Owen was testing Natalie, too, seeing

how long she would hang in there and wait for a commitment. It didn't help that Owen's parents had been through a nasty divorce when he was young, and that his dad had gone on to a couple more marriages, none of which had lasted very long.

"Owen," I asked, "did you make any decisions or adopt any beliefs about marriage and commitment as a result of your parents' divorce and your father's relationship history?" I was working to help Owen begin to get in touch with the origins of his fear of a long-term commitment and marriage.

"Marriage seems to always create conflict and lead to divorce," he said. "I have a great relationship with Natalie, the best I have ever had, so why ruin it?"

I turned to Natalie. "I want you to know that there's nothing wrong with wanting a commitment. You have every right to want that commitment. But testing Owen isn't the way to get it. In fact, it's pretty likely that it will get you exactly what you *don't* want."

"Here's what my eyes have been opened to," Owen revealed. "It might really be time for me to stop letting experiences from my past keep me from being here in the present with you and from facing my fears—disappointing you and disappointing me."

"So, Natalie, here's the crossroads that I think you're at," I said. "You love Owen, clearly, and he loves you, but the reality is that he may never change his mind. He may never be 'ready.' What I would suggest is deciding how long are you willing to stay with him without, as you say, a real commitment. Is it three months? Six months? A year?

Longer? Can you love him even if things stay exactly as they are?"

"As difficult as that seems, it makes sense," she said.

"And then at some point," I continued, "you'll be able to say to Owen, 'You know, it's been x amount of months, and I love you, but it's time for me to move on.' Do you see how that way, it's not about giving him an ultimatum? It's about *you* deciding what you're comfortable with. And really, I'm not so much worried about the testing continuing, because I think you really get it."

With most couples, resolutions aren't really arrived at in the office. It's the *understanding* that leads to a resolution that clients find on this darn sofa, which feels like the second therapist in this book. Natalie and Owen hadn't spent as much time in conflict as some of the other couples in this book, and so they didn't necessarily need to spend as much time transforming that conflict into a circle of love. When they left my office that day, there was no guarantee that Owen would ever be able to commit, and there was no guarantee that Natalie would stick with him until he was ready to make a definite decision. But once they saw the real reasons for the actions that were pulling them closer and closer to the Testing, Testing, 1, 2, 3 conflict loop, they were at least able to make the choice that was right for them—right for who they really were when they put the testing and the fear aside. And so they learned about themselves and left some important baggage behind.

REPLACE TESTING WITH ASKING

There are two ways to get information in a relationship: directly and indirectly. For example, if you want to know if your partner really loves you, you can ask . . . or you can see how many times this week your partner picks up your dirty socks from the floor by the foot of the bed. A second indirect way to get information is by testing. Sometimes testing happens in big ways: you push and push and push your partner to see how much he or she can bend before breaking. But testing can also be done in small ways, like putting the dog in the backyard instead of taking him for a walk, or drinking milk straight from the carton. You might think to yourself, *Hey, I didn't do the dishes, and she didn't get mad! I wonder how much I can get away with now.* But this kind of "little" testing can amount to death by a thousand paper cuts.

Testing can also take the form of not abiding by agreements, like not keeping the noise down when you're talking on the phone, or making other plans on a standing date night. Somewhere deep down, you know you're doing it, too. You are aware that you're testing your partner to see what happens. This 3-Minute Fix challenges you to come clean.

Instead of leaving wine bottles around the house or waiting to see if your partner notices the mounting balance on the credit cards, ask yourself what fear is motivating you to do this testing. What insecurity or anxiety is the test meant to assuage? For instance, if you are leaving wine bottles around the house, are you playing the "If you loved me, you would . . ." game? Are you thinking, *I am drinking more and more. I am worried about my drinking, are you? If you loved me, you would notice I am coming home later and later at night.*

Testing boundaries is common. Instead of testing, get the issue out in the open with your partner. Ask the questions that are on your mind. It may not be enough to ask, "Do you *really* love me?" You might need to explore with your partner why you need this reassurance, you might need to ask for help, and you might need to come up with ways that your partner can speak to you with actions as well as words. If you ask your partner directly for the answers to those questions that are dogging you, you won't need to test to get them. That takes emotional courage.

TESTING THE WATERS

What I've found in my practice over the course of the last decade is that more women than men are making the decision to leave their marriage. When a man leaves a relationship, the woman might have sensed that he was unhappy or that something or someone else was pulling him away, and so the breakup might not come as much of a surprise. But when a woman leaves, the man is often blindsided, even if for years, she had been saying things like, "I need you to talk to me. I need more. I feel like we're drifting apart. I feel lonely in this relationship." If the couple comes to therapy, the husband often doesn't treat it as a wake-up call. It's not until the woman actually packs her bags and leaves that the man realizes just how serious she is. Dan was one of those men.

Dan and his wife, Cheryl, came to see me right after the last of their three children had left home for college.

"I spent twenty-three years of marriage saying, 'Honey, why don't we do this? Honey, why don't we do that? I want us to connect more, talk more.' And it was like pulling teeth. He would say, 'Honey, you go. I just need to putter around the house, catch up on paperwork.' I stopped asking. And, truthfully, I don't want to spend the next couple of decades feeling like we're roommates," Cheryl said.

"So, Dan, what's going on with you?" I asked.

"I'm just listening," he said.

"This is what I mean," said Cheryl. "I don't have the emotional bandwidth to convince you to do things, or to pull on you until you join me. I'm tired of being the one who says, 'Hey, your dad died, and you haven't shared your feelings about it much. Do you want to talk about it?' "

"The more unavailable Dan was, the more you looked for meaning and connection outside the relationship. You were testing the waters," I said.

"But I feel like I've been pulling for so long, trying to get him to open up more, talk to me! And nothing is changing. I need more. I need to feel a deeper connection." She turned to face her husband, clearly looking for some kind of reaction. Dan placed his hands on his thighs and gave a thoughtful nod, but that was it.

"Dan, how do you feel about what Cheryl is saying?" I asked.

He exhaled. "I feel like I don't know how to give her what she wants. I want to." He turned to look at his wife. "And I know you've been saying you need more," he said.

"I want to give you that. I just . . . I don't think I know how."

"This is something a lot of men struggle with," I said. "It can be hard to find the words. And sometimes we women forget that while we love to talk about every detail, every emotion . . . that it's fun and comes naturally to us, and is a recreational sport for us, for men, it's not so much fun, and it doesn't come so easy."

Cheryl and Dan both laughed a little, and I felt some of tension in the room dissipate.

"Here's a start, Dan. And I know it's difficult, but turn to your wife and ask her, 'What can I do to make you feel like you're not so alone in this relationship?'"

He did, and Cheryl responded, "You could tell me how you're feeling."

Dan thought for a moment. "Well, I may not get this right. . . ."

"That's okay, honey," Cheryl said.

"No one's looking for perfection here," I noted. "Just take a breath, and when Cheryl says, 'I love you, and I don't want to leave, but I need more,' how do you feel? Sometimes, when it's hard to get in touch with what you're feeling, you can start by just noticing what's going on in your body."

"I'm feeling really sad," he said.

"Where do you feel that?"

"I feel it in my heart. I feel tears welling up."

"Okay, now turn to your wife."

"I realize that maybe I haven't done a great job," he said slowly. "I have definitely been complacent, even resistant. I may have taken you for granted. I may have made the assumption that you would just always be here. But losing you would break my heart."

"Dan, what else are you feeling?" I said.

"I'm just wondering if this is because you've met somebody else," he said.

"I can tell you for sure, this isn't about somebody else," Cheryl responded. "But the truth is, after years and years of asking you to come to everything, even that photography workshop, and going by myself, I *did* meet somebody else who . . . Honestly, he's just a friend. We were partnered up, and we've been doing these projects. And it's interesting, you haven't even asked me. . . . You haven't asked to see the photographs or anything. I have been spending time with him, and it's been kind of nice.

"My workshop partner went through a divorce, and he really has a lot of regrets. It's been nice talking to somebody who talks about his feelings. To be honest, I do kind of wonder what life would be like with somebody like him. Just to be really clear, when I think about moving out, I don't want to be in a relationship with him or anyone else. I just think about what life would be like living on my own. In many ways I realize I have been testing the waters these past few years. I just need to find myself."

"Do you two fight?" I asked.

"It used to be a power struggle sometimes. Now I can't say we fight. We just do our own thing. It's like a silent agreement . . . but it just feels dead to me," said Cheryl.

I said to Dan, "She's talking about having an affair of the heart with another man. How do you feel?"

"I don't know. I guess I *am* shut down," Dan said. "I

just . . . don't want you to leave me," he said through a sob.

While Dan had been walled off, Cheryl had been wondering what else was out there. Not only had she been wondering, but she'd also been testing—exploring a life without her marriage, a life without Dan. Taking the photography class and participating in a variety of other personal growth workshops was in part a way for Cheryl to find the fulfillment that was lacking in the relationship. It was also a way for Cheryl to test what the world would be like if she were on her own. What she realized was that she might be better off alone. I've seen this realization dawn on couples most often when the kids are finally out of the house. Without the distraction of focusing on the kids and all the activity, one partner suddenly gets in touch with his or her unhappiness or emptiness and acts on the awareness that there may be more out there.

Women nowadays have greater financial independence and more career opportunities than in decades past, and so when these realizations about relationship satisfaction manifest themselves, women today are more able to act on them than did women of previous generations. Cheryl was one of these women. She was saying, "I want more, and if I can't have more with you, I'd rather be alone." She had spent the past decade slowly drifting away from her marriage, and she had found the emotional courage to decide she wanted more than a roommate. Now she wasn't going to be dissuaded from seeking more by a forty-five-minute session. But she did decide to put off moving out.

"I'd like to hear his plan," she said.

"One thing I'd like to do is come to therapy every week. Can you do that?" Dan asked.

"Well, I *can*," said Cheryl. "I still feel like I'm going through the motions, but . . ."

"Do you love him?" I asked.

"I do, deep down inside, but I am not ready to say my heart is completely open," Cheryl replied.

"If you fell in love with him and stayed all these years, there had to have been more at some point, right?" I said.

Dan was quick to find words. "You were like a ray of sunshine," he said. "You were always excited about whatever was going on, were filled with so much life, excited about so many things. It was so easy to talk to you. I liked how free you were and open."

"I loved how down to earth he was," Cheryl said. "So grounded and serious, a businessman in a traditional job, but very dependable, which is what I thought I needed in the man I would spend the rest of my life with. Most of the men I dated were more artistic types . . . actors, writers. They were fun and passionate, but I started to realize they weren't the kind of man I wanted to settle down with, build a life with. Then I met Dan." She turned to him. "Then I met *you*. You got me to settle down, helped me be a bit more practical. It felt like the perfect yin and yang. But now he never seems interested anymore . . . never has the words."

"Never?" I asked.

"Well, actually, sometimes he'll write me cards or send me texts that are so beautiful and poetic and heartfelt, and I think that's what kept me going. In those moments I see the love and the tenderness . . . but I guess I still want more. Where is that man? Where is he most of the time?" Cheryl said.

"I want more of that, too," Dan said.

As with many of the couples whose stories appear in

this book, there was no neat little resolution package tied up in a bow for Dan and Cheryl. Dan was doing the best he could do, but he had become complacent and had assumed that the relationship and Cheryl would always be there. And Cheryl had spent *years* doing the best she could. What had started out as a very healthy choice to take care of herself, to make herself happy in a way that was lacking in the marriage, had turned into an affair of the heart with the man she met at the photography workshop. She had crossed a boundary.

At this point there was no guarantee that Dan's renewed commitment was going to save this marriage. But by putting their conflict loop on the table in front of them, discussing the unspoken agreements they had made with each other, and acknowledging what was at stake, Dan and Cheryl had given themselves the best damn shot they could have. Keep reading to see how you can do the same for your relationship.

3-MINUTE FIX

GIVE IT A YEAR

I always say to clients, whether they see me on an individual basis or as a couple, "Before you bail because you believe the problem is your partner, spend a year working on yourself. Learn what you can from the relationship . . . *before* you leave. Let go of the belief that you need to change your partner in order for you to be happy. Do what you need to do, within agreed-upon boundaries, to take responsibility for your own happiness."

If you are like Dan and Cheryl, in a downward spiral fueled by neglect, complacency, and hopelessness, you owe yourself that year. Do the work to continue to grow as individuals and as a couple in a way that supports moving *into* the relationship, growing together, instead of apart. If your relationship, like Dan and Cheryl's, has already lasted for so long, what's just one more year? But that doesn't mean you should just noodle through the year, as you've done in previous years of your relationship. If you're going to give it a year, do so with a plan. Cheryl ended the friendship with the man she had met in the photography workshop, the man with whom she had unwittingly been testing the waters. Although this friendship had not been sexual, it had started to cross the line, becoming an affair of the heart. A nonsexual relationship can be as damaging as a sexual one, and sometimes more so.

Consider Dan's plan to commit to therapy and to move out of his comfort zone. What commitment will you make this year to give your relationship a fighting chance? The danger here is deciding that for this year you will acquiesce to your partner's agenda. In other words, you'll give the relationship a year of compliance and see if you can make it work. But that's not an approach that you can sustain for an entire year. You need to *choose* from your heart with no guarantees to roll up your sleeves, go back to your partner, make some changes, and share experiences that nurture the relationship and yourself in the process. If you choose from your heart to make your partner happy and grow the relationship, it will never feel like acquiescing or compromising. Instead, think of things you can do over the course of a year that will create the relationship you want. Give it your best shot—put your full heart and soul into it. It may take a year to evaluate your relationship fully, but it takes only three minutes to make a commitment.

TESTING ALLIANCES

It can be hard enough in a traditional family to figure out your role, to decide, for instance, who packs the lunches, who pays the bills, and whom the kids should seek out when they skin a knee. Today, more and more families are blended families, and it can be even harder to settle into roles. Sometimes the only way to discover which roles fit is to test them. If you're a blended family, your kids will be testing, the ex will be testing, you will be testing, and the kids from your partner's previous relationships will be testing. If you can imagine the combination, you can bet there will be testing. Some testing is healthy. It's normal to wonder where you belong in a new family and to ask questions like: "Do you love your kids more than me?" "Are you still more attached to your ex, or am I number one now?"

Within this mix of testing are wonderful and positive intentions, too. For example, a new stepmom wants to be loved and accepted and is learning to set appropriate boundaries, and a new stepfather wants to show he's cool, too. But testing turns into a conflict loop when the issue of testing itself is not addressed or when the person who is testing does it simply for the sake of testing. This can be especially true of children in a blended family. The marriage might seem like a happy ending and a wonderful new beginning for you and your new spouse, but for the children, this new beginning is really built on heartache and on a situation in which they never had a vote. The children never got the choice that you got; they may not be part of your celebration.

Take Claire and Nathan, newlyweds with kids from previous marriages.

"Claire took the kids to see a movie on a school night, but my daughter Cassie hadn't done her homework. So, my ex-wife, Carol, ended up getting a call from the school the next day, and I had to hear all about it," Nathan said after taking a seat in my office. If you can untangle exactly what he means, then you're pretty well versed in the language of blended families yourself.

"She told me she had finished her homework," Claire said, visibly annoyed.

"I understand, honey, but Cassie is twelve. You can't always take her word for it."

"Okay, let's stop for a minute so I can take a little history," I said, hoping to stem the "he said, she said" debate that was unfolding right in front of me. "Why don't we back up a little bit, and you can give me a clearer picture of what's been going on?"

"Sure," Nathan said, with a sympathetic smile. "Claire and I were married almost a year ago. Claire really likes my kids. But I don't think things have been going really well lately. I think the tension's been building for a while. We moved in, got married six months ago, and it just seems like a power struggle has been building ever since. There's been more tension between Claire and my ex-wife, too."

Nathan then explained that Claire had been working really hard to get his girls to like her. Of course, the girls knew it, and they had been pushing Claire to buy them more clothes and let them stay up late. They had been attempting to push the boundaries.

"It just seems like there's a lot of confusion," Claire said.

"What kind of confusion?" I asked.

"Well," said Nathan, "Claire and I always seem to be getting our wires crossed about who's supposed to be doing what, when. Or about what the girls are and are not allowed to do. For example, Claire bought Cassie some clothes. Cassie loved them, but I guess my ex-wife had a problem. She ended up calling me, and it turned into yet another battle with me caught in the middle."

"I just wanted to do something nice for her," Claire said. "I'm trying to feel my way, to figure out how to be a good stepmom, to create some kind of connection and build a relationship with her. But I feel like sometimes you don't support me. Or that Carol gets more of your support."

"Well, I want to support you," Nathan said, looking at his wife. "But lately, I feel like you're not even around." He turned to me. "After we got engaged, and for the first few months of our marriage, Claire was always home on the nights when the girls were with us, and she would make a big family dinner. But now, most days I come home from work to an empty house. She's usually out with her friends or taking a class at the gym."

"Tara, can I just jump in here and say that his ex calls at all hours of the night, and he always ends up running over there?" Claire turned to me, clearly looking for understanding. "He'll be gone for hours, and when I call his cell phone, he'll say he ended up staying to eat dinner with the kids. Or he's fixing a leaky faucet. Or whatever. I think Carol just invents reasons to call him." She turned again to

Nathan. "You say you're caught in the middle, but I'm left here, thinking, 'Fine. I'll just do my own thing. I'll make my own plans.' I feel like I'm on my own so much of the time, anyway."

"I *am* caught in the middle. This is the mother of my children. I can't just ignore her. We're always going to be connected because of the kids."

"I'm not asking you to ignore her. I really do want you to have a good relationship with her. I just feel like these power struggles between you and me, me and the kids, and me and your ex are going to contaminate our relationship. I know you're doing your best, sweetie. It just seems like you're so worried about trying to keep Carol happy that I'm invisible. It's like Carol is more important than me."

As challenging as it is to become a blended family, Claire and Nathan weren't really fighting about the decisions Claire was making as a new stepmother or even about Nathan's ex-wife. This was about testing, too. It's common for family members to test each other as they try to discern their new roles and figure out where they fit within the expanded family. But Nathan was making the mistake that a lot of men make: because he wanted everyone to be happy—his ex-wife, his current wife, and his kids—he had been avoiding confrontation, throwing his hands up whenever he felt "caught in the middle." The result was that no one was happy. Nathan had unintentionally empowered his kids to take advantage of Claire, and his ex-wife to insert herself into his new relationship.

"Have the two of you ever talked about the challenges of this transition?" I asked. "Because it's really tough for everyone—the two of you, the kids, and for your ex, too. But this is also really normal."

Nathan shook his head. "Until recently, everything had been pretty easy. It didn't seem like there was anything left to talk about."

"Then it sounds like that is really where the work is now. For everyone in the family to work through completing the transition, so everyone can stop feeling a need to test each other. So, let me ask you, Claire. Could you turn to Nathan and explain to him what you really want? What would you really like to see happen?"

Claire adjusted herself on the sofa and reached out to touch Nathan's knee. "I just want to know that I'm important."

"You *are* important," he said.

"And I really do want to be a good stepmom. I want you to know that. I was cooking all those meals because I thought dinnertime would become this nice little routine for us, and it would help with my connection to the girls." A sly smile spread across Claire's lips. "But the truth is, I've been feeling so powerless to get you to understand what's been going on that I started letting you come home to an empty house, just to see if you noticed."

Nathan laughed. "Oh, I noticed. I think that on some level I've felt a little bit guilty about being divorced. I've been trying so hard to reassure my kids that they're loved, but I realize now that it's come at the expense of letting *you* know that."

WHAT DOES LOVE MEAN TO YOU?

As we saw in the case of Nathan and Claire, one of the challenges that partners in a blended family face is staying solid in their relationship as it is buffeted by outside forces. That's why it's so important that partners in blended families, and, in fact, in *any* family, start with a solid understanding of what love means in their relationship. A good way to start understanding what love means in your relationship is to explore what it meant in your family while you were growing up. With openness and curiosity, ask your partner the following questions:

1. What did the love between your parents look like or *not* look like? How was it expressed?
2. When one of your parents expressed affection or love to the other, what happened?
3. Based on your parents' relationship, what decisions did you make about love and what beliefs did you adopt?
4. What have you come to believe about being vulnerable, about extending or receiving love?
5. What decisions did you make in past relationships about giving love or being loved?
6. What were the results of those decisions? Which of your previous decisions turned out to be good, healthy choices, and which were not so healthy? Does this affect your willingness to make these same choices again?
7. When, if ever, did you let yourself be vulnerable in a previous relationship? What happened?

8. Fill in the blank: If I allow myself to be 100 percent present to your love, _____.

9. Fill in the blank: Something I do to be less lovable is_____
_____.

10. What would happen if you allowed yourself to love me deeply?

HEARTwork

Transforming Testing, Testing, 1, 2, 3 into Profound Trust

Exercise 1: The Testing, Testing, 1, 2, 3 Quiz

Are you in a Testing, Testing, 1, 2, 3 conflict loop? To find out, read the following statements, and for each one, circle the number for the response that comes closest to how you feel.

1 = Strongly Disagree, 2 = Disagree, 3 = Agree, 4 = Strongly Agree

1. I avoid asking for what I want, and I test the waters instead.

   1   2   3   4

2. I have tested the relationship via my physical or emotional involvement with others (e.g., ex-lovers, people I am attracted to).

   1   2   3   4

3. Eventually, it seems like one of us will have to give in.

   1   2   3   4

4. When my partner sets boundaries, it feels like an open invitation to test them.

   1   2   3   4

5. Asking my partner directly for what I need just seems too scary.

    1   2   3   4

6. We test each other so much that it's started to feel like a game.

    1   2   3   4

7. I can't get a real answer from my partner, so I might as well get an indirect one by testing.

    1   2   3   4

8. I want to know if my mate really loves me . . . but asking isn't an option.

    1   2   3   4

9. Sometimes I like provoking my mate, just because I know that I can.

    1   2   3   4

10. I catch myself doing things I know my partner disapproves of.

    1   2   3   4

11. If I can get my partner a little "riled up," it helps me relax.

    1   2   3   4

12. I flirt with others when I know that my partner is watching.

    1   2   3   4

13. When my partner doesn't do what I want, I find subtle ways to get payback.

    1   2   3   4

14. I worry that my partner will leave me, but I don't know if I should really be worried or not.

    1   2   3   4

15. Sometimes I say one thing when I really mean another.

| | 1 | 2 | 3 | 4 |

16. I don't know why I can't just trust in my partner's love.

| | 1 | 2 | 3 | 4 |

17. I like surprising my partner with little hoops that he or she has to jump through to earn my affection.

| | 1 | 2 | 3 | 4 |

18. I like to keep in touch with old flames just to know where they are. Or I worry that my partner is keeping in touch with old flames.

| | 1 | 2 | 3 | 4 |

19. I'm totally confused. Why can't we just get along?

| | 1 | 2 | 3 | 4 |

20. It feels like we're both jockeying for the "lead" position in this relationship, trying to get one up on the other.

| | 1 | 2 | 3 | 4 |

Scoring: Add up the numbers you circled for your total score.

Below 35: You're not testing, and your partner isn't necessarily testing, either. This doesn't mean that you're not in a conflict loop; it means that you're probably not in this one. You may have seen parts of yourself in this chapter, but there's a good chance you'll see more of yourself and your relationship in other chapters. Keep reading.

35–50: It's hard for you to believe in your partner's commitment to you or ability to accept you for who you are. You need reassurance. And you get this reassurance through testing. Use the following

HEARTwork exercises to help you identify healthier ways to find this affirmation.

51 or above: For whatever reason, you don't believe in your partner or in yourself. You're so incredulous when it comes to your relationship that you design opportunity after opportunity for you or your partner to fail. If you or your partner can pass every test, the relationship can keep going. But it seems like it would take just one slipup for the whole thing to come tumbling down. In addition to completing the following HEARTwork exercises, consider working with a professional who can help guide your transformation.

Exercise 2: Get to the Root of Why You Test

We all test, and some tests are actually good. You may test yourself to see if you can manage ten more crunches or resist eating that last cupcake, which has been calling your name. Other types of testing, however, may be keeping you from what you most want: love, peace, and a renewed sense of connection with your partner. Exploring the conflict may prove to be a path to understanding.

Consider the following questions on your morning run or while having an afternoon cup of tea, and just wait for the answers to come on their own. You may instead choose to address them head-on all in one sitting. Let thoughts, images, and even memories bubble up in your mind, and record your answers or journal about them on paper or electronically. If you wish, you can even draw whatever arises in you. Remember, no one needs to know your answers to these questions except you. Share these insights only if you wish to and when you are ready.

1. How have you been testing your spouse or partner? These can be big tests (drinking too much) or small ones ("forgetting"

to mow the lawn). Leave your judgment behind and simply explore your actions.

2. Thinking as far back as childhood, can you remember a specific time when you realized that you could (or even had to) test someone in order to get your needs met? Did a specific event precipitate this?

3. Did this testing get you the result you wanted? What happened as a result of your testing?

4. What was the decision you made about testing (e.g., "It's the only way I know to get what I want" or "It's the only way to get him to see how valuable I am").

5. In your current relationship, what is the story you told yourself about why you need to test? Are you testing as a way to reassure yourself of something unrelated to your partner? Is the testing getting you the results you want? Are you looking to someone else to fix something that can be fixed only by you?

6. How has your testing behavior affected your spouse or partner? Your relationship?

7. Are you willing to face whatever the fear is underneath your testing behavior?

Exercise 3: Discover the Loving Behavior

You feel like your partner may be testing you, but are you sure? The only way to find out is to name the elephant in the room. It might take saying something like "I'm wondering . . . are you *really* interested in your ex, or are you testing me?" or "Why does it seem like you're seeing how far you can push me before I break?"

There's another elephant in the room, and that's what *you* get from allowing yourself to be tested. Do you secretly or uncon-sciously collude with your partner's testing because you don't want to face an issue? Often we choose not to see what we see or know what we know in the erroneous belief that it will simply go away or will resolve itself on its own. It may also be that we aren't willing to muster the emotional courage to take the actions or make the nec-essary decisions that come with facing the truth, telling ourselves we don't want to make our partner uncomfortable, when in reality we are afraid of our own discomfort. Or are you testing your partner to see how far he or she will go with it? You might even want to see how much rope you can give your partner so that your partner can hang him- or herself. So, what's your hope or expectation? If you continue to pass these tests, what will happen? Will your partner stop testing? Will he or she learn a lesson? Will he or she take re-sponsibility for what happens next?

Imagine that you're all alone. Nobody's listening, and nobody's judging. In your heart of hearts, do you sense that your actions to-ward yourself or toward your partner are loving? Ask yourself what the loving behavior would be. For example, if there's a lot of drink-ing going on, can you say in a loving, nonjudgmental way, "Honey, I'm a little worried about your drinking. Do you want to talk about it?" Or if it's another issue, can you say, "You've been dressing a little more provocatively and leaving your phone on, with texts from your ex on the screen, where I can see them. Are you feeling anx-ious about our commitment together? Do you want to talk about it?" Instead of doing some testing yourself, now is the time to take a mindful moment, muster your emotional courage to ask, and act in a loving way to support your partner's and your own physical, spiritual, and emotional growth.

Chapter 7

● ● ● ● ● ● ●

Grow Apart ∞
Grow Together

S OME PEOPLE JUMP into the process of learning and growing. It's in their DNA, and they find it exciting. There's
always a workshop to attend or a novel food to try or some-
place new to visit. This first type of person may have been
a naturally exuberant child who always sought out new
adventures. Whereas other people are like, "I don't want to
leave my comfort zone!" This second type of person may
have started off as an exuberant child or even discovered
this part of him- or herself later as an adult only to be given
the message to tone it down or play it safe. Joseph Campbell so famously said, "Follow your bliss," but for this second type of person, it's easier said than done. Where and
how do we find our passion? Start with one of the main
ingredients of a healthy relationship—namely, curiosity.
That's it. Keep it simple. With curiosity often comes pas-

sion, a new direction, and growth. Try asking your partner and yourself questions like: Why do you feel that way? Why do you believe that way? Where does this belief come from? What's the worst that can happen if you engage your partner in this manner?

Whether you are naturally exuberant—always seeking the next new adventure—or more reserved, change also comes about simply with time, since growing is inevitable. Sometimes things happen, external things, that force you to grow whether you like it or not: A parent dies. Your partner, who you thought was going to have that secure job you planned your life around, gets laid off. Your young, healthy wife gets diagnosed with breast cancer. Your plans to start a family end after rounds and rounds of fertility treatment. Or result in triplets. As you confront this event, you know that your path is going to change. You either embrace change and reframe it and look at new choices . . . or you end up stuck.

A loving, enduring relationship is in part an evolving relationship, meaning that the people in it keep evolving individually and also as a couple. It's this growing together that keeps the excitement and the interest and even the sexual passion alive. Think about how often people say, "I just outgrew him" or "I got involved with this woman because she was exciting." Whether it's job layoffs or environmental crises, living in vulnerable times adds to the fragility of our intimate relationships. And there's always that one particular question that comes up at various points in our lives: "Is this all there is?" Sometimes our answer is "If so, maybe I need more, and maybe I need to make some radical changes."

It's inevitable: couples are either going to grow together or grow apart. And don't kid yourself. If you haven't yet had to deal with important life issues, the kind that test a relationship, you will. Will you be able to say, "We survived the job loss, we survived breast cancer, and we are still teammates, and we're stronger than before"? Or will you be unable to handle the changes . . . and decide to bail? In other words, will you have grown together or grown apart?

You have the opportunity to strengthen your relationship in this chapter, and I will show you how. This is the chance to reframe, and to step up and show your partner, what is important to you. Your memories are the glue that strengthens a relationship when minor stuff comes up. In this chapter we'll also look toward the future, with the sincere hope that what happens next will be even better than the memories you've already made with your partner.

You don't have to do exactly the same thing in order to grow together. So you both don't have to come to love scuba diving or Proust. You just need to keep growing individually in ways you both can respect and appreciate. For instance, my husband, Eric, voraciously listens to audiobooks, especially biographies about presidents and historical figures, such as Winston Churchill, whereas I love novels and am a voracious reader of fiction. It is my healthy escape!

Well, we were making dinner one night, and he was telling me about the Bob Dylan biography he was listening to. He was familiar with only a few songs; I knew most of them by heart. He would mention a song in the biography, and I would break into song. So there I was, singing Dylan songs. Fortunately, by some miracle, my husband loves listening to me sing. We were chopping vegetables, laughing like crazy, doing our thing. Fun! Remember, the trick isn't to agree on everything or do exactly the same things or even appreciate the same things. It's to keep growing. If one person is growing and doing new things, while the other stays stuck, that's when you grow apart.

DESIGNING A NEW SELF

Tom and Susan grew up in a small town in Iowa. Tom's dad was a foreman at the John Deere factory, and Susan's dad made a living as the owner of a franchise hotel. Susan's mother made sure Susan and her four siblings were on the school bus, with snacks and homework in hand. All four parents had been married since they were in their early twenties, and while Tom and Susan waited to get married until Tom was twenty-eight and Susan twenty-six, they were high school sweethearts. For the most part, Tom and Susan had lived life within the limits that their parents and their surroundings had set for them. Out of high school, Tom took a job in heavy equipment sales, and with hard work, he started climbing the ladder of pay raises and promotions. Soon after they married, Susan got pregnant with their first child.

During the pregnancy, one of Tom's high school friends offered him a position managing a harvesting equipment dealership in Santa Rosa, California. With the money their parents had pooled together as a loan to cover the down payment, Tom and Susan bought a two-bedroom house with a small backyard garden in a neighborhood of Petaluma, just a couple of miles south of where Tom would be working. The couple packed everything they needed to start a new life into a U-Haul truck and drove due west on I-80, stopping just before they would've gotten their feet wet in the Pacific Ocean. Later, Susan told me the drive was one of the best moments in their relationship—just her—and the baby growing inside her—and Tom, talking about their hopes and dreams as the miles spooled away under the truck's tires. They were nervous but excited, and anything seemed possible. Most importantly, they were in it together. But some things went without saying. Tom would manage the equipment business and maybe even own one someday, while Susan would raise the family's children, just as her mother had done.

Susan had the baby, a beautiful little girl named Grace. Susan's parents had planned to fly in to help right after the baby arrived, but a couple of days before the birth, her father had called to say that Susan's mother was a little sick and didn't want the new mom or the baby to catch the bug. "We'll come next month," he'd promised. A month later, Susan called to check on their plans, and her dad suggested that once the baby was able to travel, Susan and Tom could come to visit Susan's parents in Iowa instead. Susan knew right away that something was wrong. She and the baby were on the next flight home. They arrived just in time to see Susan's mother before she was scheduled for heart surgery to correct, for a time, clogged arteries in her heart.

Before the surgery, Susan's mother smiled at her and

Grace and said, "Sweetheart, I'm sure I'll be fine. But I want you to promise me—promise me you'll live your dream. Do what your heart tells you to do."

Susan's mother never woke up from the surgery. Tom flew in for the funeral, and then the young family flew back to California. Tom returned to his job in Santa Rosa, and Susan's life revolved around Grace and their small house in Petaluma. And that's when Susan started feeling depressed. Tom understood. After all, Susan's mother had just passed. But when one month of depression stretched to two and then stretched to three, Tom started wondering how long it would take Susan to "snap out of it," as he later told me. He suggested they start trying for a second child, and he encouraged Susan to join a knitting group (knitting was a hobby she had always enjoyed). When she spoke to her ob-gyn, he gave her the business card of a local therapist instead: me.

Susan tucked the card away, knowing Tom wouldn't like the idea of therapy. Instead, she agreed to a second child, and they started trying, though she later told me that her heart wasn't in it and she secretly hoped she wouldn't get pregnant. "I don't know what's wrong with me," she said much later. "I have this beautiful child, a loving husband. Why can't I just be happy?" Mostly to please her husband and show she was trying, Susan also joined a knitting circle. She didn't have any friends out West, and she decided that maybe the company of other women would do her some good.

Now, I'm not quite sure what knitting circles are like in the rest of the country, but in the Bay Area, they aren't like your mother's needlepoint group. One Wednesday evening, Susan left baby Grace with a kind neighbor and drove a couple of minutes east to Sonoma for a knitting circle she'd seen advertised on a flyer at the grocery store. Susan knew immediately that she wasn't in Kansas or Iowa anymore. The group met at the home of two gay moms who were in a deeply committed relationship and who worked in the wine industry. The women in the group were young, old, single, and married. They were stay-at-home moms and moms with full-time jobs, plus a seventy-five-year-old artist who still painted every day. The knitting was good, the wine was better, but it was the conversation that really lifted Susan's spirits.

Susan started feeling better immediately, and Tom thought his advice had really done the trick. That lasted for about two weeks. Then Tom started asking Susan how long she thought the neighbor would be willing to watch Grace every Wednesday and what he was supposed to do about dinner those nights. Couldn't Susan just knit at home? When Susan pushed back, the conflict started. When she came home one Wednesday evening with a course catalog for the local college, Tom started panicking.

"Are you kidding me?" he said. "What happened to our plan?"

"I love you. I love Grace. But I don't want to end up like my mother," Susan said. "I want to talk to someone who can help us."

Tom asked her why they should tell their problems to a stranger. He said it wouldn't do any good. He complained about the cost. But eventually, he agreed to join Susan for just one session, with the condition that she not tell anyone and that if he wasn't comfortable, he never had to go again. That was when Susan pulled out the business card that had been sitting in her sock drawer for four months and the couple first visited my office.

To Susan's surprise, and maybe to Tom's as well, after we introduced ourselves, Tom volunteered to go first. "Well, Tara," he began, "I don't know what's wrong with my wife. Everything was fine, and then her mom died and she joined this . . . *knitting group.*"

"Are you sure everything was fine?" I asked.

Susan immediately started crying.

"I guess . . . I guess maybe not," he said. It was obvious that Tom was traditional, but he was also smart and competent. "But we come from a place where you do what your parents did. It was simple, and things worked out just fine. It's not like anyone in our family or circle of friends ever got divorced. I don't understand."

Susan said that she loved her husband, but she made it very clear that she planned to keep going to the knitting group. Admitting that he didn't have the answers was an encouraging first step for Tom: it allowed him to start asking the right questions. Tom wasn't a man to duck his problems. He faced things head-on and with hard work, and he brought the same approach to couples therapy. In that room, he proved that he was committed to doing whatever it took to save his marriage and repair his relationship with his wife, whom he did truly love.

For Susan and Tom, repairing the relationship entailed exploring each partner's role. This is the case for many couples. Sure, Tom and Susan represent traditional gender roles, but we all have our programming, our beliefs and conditioning. Once you separate from your parents, your childhood friends, and maybe even the subculture that comes with geography, you have the opportunity to challenge those beliefs from childhood or from society. You have the opportunity to create your own family and your own role within it. Just like giving birth, creating a new, independent self can be painful, and you may encounter resistance. This resistance to change can come from within, as a result of feeling like you're unmoored from what you know and floating aimlessly, facing questions you never even thought to ask. Or this resistance can come from your partner, who understood you to have one set of values and beliefs and now must confront the reality that suddenly you have evolved and have an entirely different set. The underlying fear is that you are growing apart as a couple. Your partner is thinking, *Are you growing away from me? Will you grow out of love with me?*

"You find the right girl, you get married, you have kids, you love each other, and that's that. That's happiness," Tom said.

"I believe that, too. That's who I am, too," Susan said. But then she explained that as she looked back, she didn't believe her mom had ever been truly happy. When she was growing up, every once in a while Susan caught her mother crying when her mother thought no one was watching. Susan didn't know why and didn't tell anyone, not even her siblings. "I just decided to never think about the times I caught my mom crying. Until now," Susan said. "You may get really angry or hate me for saying this, but I don't want to end up like that. I'm really thinking that in another six months, I want to start taking some classes."

"Why?" Tom asked.

"I don't know why," said Susan. "All I know is that I'm growing, and I want to keep growing."

"You know, Tom, you're in a whole new environment, too," I said. "This is an opportunity for you, too. You want life to be like it was before—before your baby was born, before your wife lost her mother, before you moved out here. Maybe you can find a way to do something for yourself on that night that Susan is out. You must be lonely."

"You know, there are a lot of guys at work, and they go out together. But I always say I have to go home. Maybe I can join them next time. . . ."

"What's something big and bold the two of you can do together to embrace this new world?" I asked.

Tom thought for a moment. "Maybe we could have a barbecue and invite your friends from the knitting group and mine from work?" he said. "But . . . does this mean everything is going to change?"

"No, of course not," I said. "The great thing is that you two still have the same values. Those haven't changed, and they're an important part of this relationship. And, Tom, you can feel really good about yourself. I believe you gave your wife a gift that was bigger than you even realized."

"What's that?" he said.

We talked about the fact that companionship and a new point of view weren't the only things Susan got from the knitting circle Tom had encouraged her to attend in the first place.

"Tell Tom what you get from your circle beyond the knitting," I said.

Susan shared how the women she had met gave her mothering exactly when she needed it most, and when she brought Grace to the knitting group occasionally, it was as if Grace had an entire gaggle of grandmothers. Their encouragement had brought Susan along in a way that neither she nor Tom could have anticipated.

"You did that for me, Tom, and I love you for that. I really don't know how I would have survived the loss of my mother, along with being a new mom, the move, everything, if I didn't have this group. I can't even imagine the kind of wife and mother I would have been without their support."

With this new understanding, Tom realized he was getting what he really wanted—a content and happy wife. He and Susan had a second child. After a year of going to school part-time, Susan started toward a nursing degree. Tom's old anxieties came up, but they were able to examine them and challenge them together. The happiness Tom felt at seeing his wife, daughter, and new son blossom took precedence over his fears. Susan loved her new responsibilities, and she loved her husband for supporting her decisions. Hey, Tom even started looking forward to his standing Wednesday night date with his kids, and he learned a few basic recipes to feed himself and the kids while Susan was away.

3-MINUTE FIX ♡

ROLE REVERSAL

When you put your partner in a box, you limit yourself; when you clip your partner's wings, you keep yourself in a cage. This means that if you strive to keep your partner confined to a single, simple role—one sometimes defined by gender—then you are ensuring that you are stuck in the single, simple role opposite your partner's.

Whatever your roles are, for this 3-Minute Fix, try reversing them. This can include swapping little chores, like folding the clothes instead of doing the dishes. Or it could mean switching places in terms of who gets the kids ready for school in the morning or who cooks dinner at night. Switching roles forces you to explore with your partner what those roles actually entail . . . and this might enable you to visualize alternatives.

3-MINUTE FIX ♡

BROADENING YOUR HORIZONS

My husband, Eric, is more adventurous than me when it comes to physical challenges, and I tend to be more adventurous when it comes to other areas in our life. To preempt a power struggle, we came up with this agreement: If there's something the other one wants to try, you make an agreement to try it once. If you hate it, you never have to do it again.

For example, remember when the Giants made it to the World Series? I could tell Eric wanted to tell me about them, and I could tell that he wanted me to sit down and watch a game with him, perhaps even muster up a little enthusiasm for his beloved San Francisco Giants. I had no interest in baseball, but when I sat down and watched a game, I became so hooked that now, whether he's here or not, I don't miss a single game. The same thing happened to Eric. I really knew he would love this wonderful group I do yoga with. He tried it just once, and he got hooked.

You can't expect your partner to make extreme changes or even the changes you want him or her to make. But if you have reasonable expectations, your partner might make small changes on your behalf. For example, I'm a vegan, and Eric isn't, but now he eats more of a plant-based diet. Commit to being flexible, moving out of your comfort zone, and giving whatever your partner wants to share with you a *try*. And if you're the one hoping for change, celebrate the changes your partner does make, even if they aren't radical.

REDEFINING GOALS AND VALUES

It's no secret that losing a job can be a traumatic, life-altering experience. And it's especially traumatic if your identity is wrapped up in your career. The fact is that the more traumatic a job loss is for one partner, the more traumatic it is for the other partner, too. Such a change creates ripples through the whole family. A job loss leaves a host of crucial questions in its wake. The most obvious one is what the person who lost the job is going to do now. Is he or she going to head right back out and look for a job like the one that was lost? Or is the job loss a wake-up call that it might be time to try something new?

This time of soul-searching can be terrifying for the newly unemployed person's partner. Hopefully, there are some savings to fall back on, but regardless, looking out at a financially insecure future can be like having a staring contest with anxiety. For this partner, the situation can be even more terrifying because there might be nothing he or she can *do* about it. The job-seeking partner is the one who surfs the Internet, looking for a new job, and actively seeks out new opportunities. It can be hard to watch as you bite your fingernails and play the waiting game.

But this "existential" crisis sometimes plays second fiddle to the new challenges of day-to-day life. Boy, wouldn't it be great to have your partner around the house all the time! However, what seems like an opportunity can quickly prove to be a challenge. Or at least it forces a family to rethink and redesign and remake its routines. If the Swiss watch has been running one way for a long time, another person "helping out" can be more like a monkey wrench in the gears.

That's what it was like for Alex and Hannah. They came to me after Alex was laid off from his job as a stockbroker, along with his whole division. By the time they visited my office, Alex had been out of work for six months. Before Alex's layoff, Hannah had lived a stay-at-home-mom lifestyle that included Pilates in Lululemon outfits and shopping at Whole Foods. Now they were burning through their savings, and the bottom of the bank account was in sight. Rather than beating the pavement or working his contacts to land a new gig, Alex was hanging around the house with his family.

"I think I used to love my job," Alex said at the beginning of our session. "At one time. Maybe when I was younger. But this is the first time I've been away from it, and I feel like I have this opportunity now, and I want to take a step back. These past few months, I've spent more time with the children than at any other point in their lives. I don't want things to go back to how they were. I don't see why that's such a bad thing," he explained, turning to face Hannah.

"I know how hard it is when a man loses his job," said Hannah, "but I'm really getting anxious. He doesn't seem to have a plan. I'm afraid he thinks this is some kind of vacation. He's home, hanging around the house all day. Or he's trying to get me to run errands with him. Or he's following me around and asking me what I have to do and offering to run errands for me. I think a reasonable amount of time has passed, and now it seems like it's time to figure things out."

"Listen, I really try to be helpful. I try to run errands and help with the kids, that kind of stuff," Alex said. "And I feel like you're saying you don't even want me around. You're treating me like I'm a pest, or like I'm always underfoot."

"When Alex was laid off, I knew some things were going to change," Hannah said to me. "But what's really scaring me is that he started talking about how he might not want to be a stockbroker anymore. He's been a broker for twenty-five years, and he's never questioned his career choice before. I can understand if he's feeling a little depressed, but when he starts talking like this, I just feel really scared. I don't know how to explain this sudden about-face. And that's why we're here."

What Hannah left unsaid was the fact that Alex seemed

to have lost all his motivation. He had gone straight into finance after college and then into trading and had climbed aggressively in his company . . . and now, if he didn't have to run out for a gallon of milk in the morning, he might not get out of his pajamas until noon.

"Why else do you think having Alex around the house is challenging for you?" I asked Hannah.

"Well, when I *see* him, it reminds me of why he's there. Sometimes when he's out running an errand or doing things, it's like I don't have to remember that he doesn't have a job. It's not like I trick myself into believing everything's all right again, but it's not like the pressure is right there, right in front of me," she said.

Remember when we talked in earlier chapters about the antidote to the "When, Then" game being to *act* a certain way and the *feelings* would follow? Well, that's true not just for a couple but for individuals, as well. Here's the thing: Alex was depressed. Yes, he was enjoying the time to do some soul-searching, but he was doing it while unshaven and in his pajamas. He had slowed down, his life had slowed down, and everything felt like it was covered by a heavy blanket. For Alex, and for many people who find they have too much time in the day and not enough things to fill it, one important thing to do is to *act* and to expect the *feelings* to follow. Just move. Find a reason to stay busy, stay motivated, and stay *moving*.

"I think maybe the first step is to work on getting some kind of routine back," I offered. I talked with Alex about the importance of keeping a schedule, of getting up at the same time every morning, of showering and getting dressed at a set time. He mentioned in response a shared work space where guys his age and younger rented desks on the cheap and dreamed up harebrained schemes for new companies, new products, new opportunities . . . some of which tanked and some of which were bought by bigger fish for money that made a couple of years of trading look like pocket change. It was a start-up community, and when Alex talked about it, I saw a light in his eyes that wasn't there when he discussed looking for another job as a stockbroker. Alex wasn't exactly sitting on an idea for the next great tech start-up, so we explored how he could get involved. One idea we came up with was having him volunteer to give a lecture at the shared work space about his area of expertise: how to invest and how to court investment.

Alex nodded. "That makes sense. I don't want to be floating around forever. I just said that I don't know if I want to go back to being a broker, but I absolutely want to go back to work full time."

I could tell that simply *talking* about what Alex would do next made Hannah more comfortable.

"Here's what's really important," I said. "I want to acknowledge how scary it is when you two have planned a life like this and now it's all changed. It's important not to minimize this change. But it's also a life challenge that could strengthen the relationship. That means both of you are going to have to work to see this as an opportunity."

Alex nodded as I spoke; Hannah still looked a little skeptical. Before the layoff, the family had never wanted for anything material. They'd enjoyed iPads, vacations, private schools. But according to Richard A. Easterlin, the happiness we get from *stuff* is temporary and fades quickly. This layoff was a chance not only for Alex to find a creative way off the treadmill that he'd been on since college, but also for the family to reframe how it defined *happiness*.

"Look," I said. "You have your health, you have each other, and you have two great kids. It's time to stop focusing on everything you *don't* have after this layoff and to start looking at everything you *do* have."

"Yeah, for years and years, Alex worked so hard, and he has really done a great job providing. I've heard about other husbands who are laid off, and they go off and play golf. At least Alex is using this as time with his kids. You know what? I think this whole private school thing—we have such smart kids—I think it's a little bit of a status thing to say my kids are in private school. I think I really want to let that one go," Hannah said.

"We usually go away for the holidays," Alex explained. "But we had to dip into the vacation fund to cover camp costs. . . ."

"How about a road trip to the Grand Canyon or Yosemite?" said Hannah. "We've been to these exotic places, but not to these things in our backyard."

We talked, too, about Hannah's career possibilities. She'd been a stay-at-home mom for so long that she had a hard time seeing herself in any other role. But she had a teaching license, which, despite Hannah's being out of the workforce for a decade, she had made sure to keep renewing.

"Maybe it's time for me to get out of my comfort zone as a private school mom. As a matter of fact, I would enjoy getting out of that mini 'rat race' and giving my days more meaning, as well as adding income to our family," she said. "Maybe I could look into being a substitute teacher."

The key for both Hannah and Alex was realizing that change was both possible and filled with opportunity. They didn't have to be the people they had always been, and in fact, life had made sure they wouldn't stay in their comfortable roles. They had spent six months looking back at what they had had in the past, and now, for the first time, they were both starting to look forward into the future. Alex was ready to reach out and grab something. He was ready to seize the opportunity before him to employ his business and financial expertise to be part of something created from scratch in that shared start-up work space. And Hannah was ready to let go of all the material things in their lives that didn't really matter and refocus her energy on the things that gave their lives meaning. She opted for *presence* instead of presents. Was redesigning their lives and their identities a safe choice? No. But this moment of change and growth was a major opportunity to create more meaningfulness in their lives and their family relationships.

3-MINUTE FIX

CONSIDER WHAT REALLY MATTERS

For Alex and Hannah, it was easy to find meaning in *things* instead of experiences. This is true for many couples. You think about how important it is for your child to have a laptop or how much better the house would look with a new kitchen or how cool it would be to take a big vacation next summer. But when you think about it, you realize you pay for these things with time. Sure, if you have a job you love or if you are helping people, the time you spend working may be deeply meaningful. But if not, it might be time to think about these *things* that control your life. Here's what I suggest: start from the opposite side. Think about the traditions that have meaning for you as a couple or as a family. These might include pressing cider in the fall, giving away all the books you have read to friends who you think will like them, volunteering to serve a meal to the homeless on Thanksgiving, or running around the yard in bare feet on the morning of the year's first snow. In your head or, better yet, on paper, make a list of these traditions.

Once you have a list of your traditions, try to set them in stone. *These* are the things that really matter to you and in your relationship. When it comes down to it, your traditions are how you define your family and your relationship.

AND BABY MAKES THREE

One of the greatest opportunities to grow and change together (or risk drifting apart) arises when a couple has children. Rich and Laurie, first-time parents to their three-month-old son, Liam, were like many new couples I've counseled over the years: a little worse for wear and seriously short on sleep. Laurie, however, had taken to motherhood like a duck to water. It was her husband she was concerned about.

"Ever since we had the baby, he has just seemed so shut down," she said. "He seems totally disinterested, almost like he doesn't even want to be a dad. I thought we were on the same page, and that he was really excited. I don't understand what's going on."

As Laurie poured out her feelings, I watched Rich shrink into the sofa, fold his hands in his lap, and gradually disengage, until he was quietly staring at a spot on the rug.

"I'm wondering, Rich, what's going on with you," I said gently. "Where do you go when you start looking down at the floor? What are you thinking?"

"I don't really want to say."

"Is there anything we can do—or that I can do—to make it safe for you to express how you're feeling?" I asked.

Rich turned to face his wife. "I want to know that you're not going to be . . . *mad* when we leave here."

Laurie nodded and took a breath. "Okay."

"And I want to know that whatever happens today, we're going to come back," he added.

Laurie was fine with that, too. "I promise," she said.

Satisfied, Rich sat up a bit in his seat. "It's not that I don't want to be a father. I adore Liam. I would do anything for him. But things are changing so fast, I feel like I can't catch my breath. I have tried to talk about this with you, but it's like you have this timetable. Or this *agenda*. I know you're already starting to think about Liam's little brother or sister and how we need a bigger house."

"Agenda?" she said, incredulous. "I don't understand. Isn't this exactly what we planned? Isn't this what people do? You get engaged. You get married. You have children."

"All I want is for things to slow down a little bit," Rich replied.

Laurie threw her hands in the air. "We'd never move forward if I left things up to you."

"I'm wondering," I said, hoping to ease the growing tension. "Did the two of you spend any time talking about how things would change when you became parents? Did you talk at all about what your roles would be? Did you talk about your hopes and fears, or your dreams for the future?"

Laurie and Rich stared at each other, with a blank look on both their faces.

"Okay," I said. "I think that may be part of the problem. Could you tell me a little more about how you *thought* things would be? What did you expect?"

"Well . . . I love my father," Rich said, "but I always thought that when I became a dad, I would do things differently."

"How so?" I asked.

"I wanted to have a relationship with my son. My dad was always around . . . you know, home every night by six. But he was never really *there*. He was more concerned about work than anything else. He wasn't someone who I had much of a connection with."

"And you would like you and your son to be close?"

He nodded. "But instead, I feel exactly like my father. I feel like I'm behaving exactly the way he always did, and I can't explain it. *I* don't even understand why I'm doing the things that I'm doing."

"Let me just take a moment to reassure both of you that this is actually really common," I said. "In my experience, when a man feels like he doesn't know what to do, he's more likely to step back and disengage than risk making a mistake."

Rich nodded enthusiastically. "That's definitely true. It's not that I don't want to help Laurie, or that I don't want to spend time with Liam, but sometimes I feel like he prefers his mom to me."

"That's normal," I said. "She's where the milk comes from. But that will change eventually. Meanwhile, the cure is to spend more time—not less—with him."

"And I know I don't always do it right," he added. "Laurie has her own ways of doing things, from diapers to bath time to whatever."

"And you'll find your own way of doing those things. And Laurie will be fine with that. Right, Laurie?" I asked.

She laughed. "I could probably stand to loosen up my standards. And I do want help. I want to feel like I have a partner. I don't want to raise our kids by myself."

"Okay, great," I said. "What kind of help? What are some things that Rich could do?"

"Maybe get on the floor and play with Liam when I'm making dinner. Or take him for a walk in the stroller when I'm really tired and need a nap."

"Do you help with the baby often?" I asked Rich. "Do you burp him or feed him or change him?"

Laurie shot me a half smile and rolled her eyes. "I pretty much do it all myself."

"Then let's start there. Rather than just expecting Rich to know what you need, why don't we come up with some kind of routine? For example, maybe after a feeding, it'll be Rich's job to burp Liam and put him to sleep. Or, maybe he could officially take over bath time duties."

Laurie heaved a giant sigh. "That would be *wonderful*."

"I can do that," Rich said, chiming in, already much more animated than I had ever seen him.

I smiled. "Okay, what else?"

"Well, I usually go out on Sunday morning to get the paper and pick up breakfast at our favorite bagel place. Maybe I could take Liam with me. That would give Laurie a break, and it'd be, like, something special that Liam and I get to do together."

As Laurie and Rich continued talking, I began to see dramatic changes in their body language—they had sat on opposite sides of the couch when they arrived at my office, and now they were turned toward each other and were coming together as a team. Laurie and Rich had successfully reframed their conflict. Now, as they focused on what kind of parents they wanted to be, the conversation flowered. It was clear from his body language that Rich was already feeling some relief from his anxiety. Meanwhile, Laurie was feeling more connected to her husband.

Change can become so overwhelming that we start to feel powerless, like our life is spinning around us and we don't have any control. We're not powerless in the face of change, however. But getting through life's challenges requires couples to come together as a team, to communicate, and to reframe any conflicts. In Rich and Laurie's case, their challenges were heightened by the fact that the things they took for granted didn't match. They were the perfect example of having unspoken expectations. Laurie had assumed that they would have kids right away. Rich hadn't necessarily agreed. But both of them had been silent about their expectations, and that was when resentment started to build.

That's one reason I am a big believer in premarital counseling, even if you're not planning a formal walk down the aisle. Premarital counseling, which can be as short as four sessions, is an opportunity to discuss the core issues that plague couples. It's a chance to discuss the in-laws, finances, parenting, the issue of whether one of you will stay at home or you'll both keep working, private or public school education, and religion. Couples have a tendency to assume that issues will work themselves out on their own (I've heard such claims as "He will change his mind once we are married" or "She'll convert once the kids come along"), and so they forgo premarital counseling, but so often, I have seen these expectations blow up in couples' faces.

Not only is it advantageous to start the conversation about your expectations and beliefs early, but it is also important to keep it going. Expectations change. Life events, like the loss of a parent, an illness, or the birth of a child, as well as more subtle changes, like developing an aversion for previous eating habits, can mean that what was once true has changed. Don't wait for your partner to bring up a topic or to continue the conversation. The more you address your expectations, the more these conversations will become organic and natural.

I gave Laurie and Rich a home assignment before they left my office. I asked them each to spend some time alone thinking of six qualities they wanted to have as parents, six qualities they wanted to give to Liam—things like the gift of compassion, the gift of being present, the gift of being curious, or the gift of being a patient teacher. The next step was to compile a list of those qualities on a piece of paper. Then I instructed them to come together to create a master list—what I call a Parent's Playbook—by incorporating ideas from each of their individual lists. Sometimes, the simple act of writing out your expectations can shine light on your *unspoken* expectations. In this case, the expectations that needed airing were around parenting.

Bringing up unspoken expectations as a couple, saying, "Here's how I thought it would be," will give you a chance to work together to *decide* how things actually will be, just as Rich and Laurie did. It's important in all relationships to share your dreams, even if they seem impractical or trigger fears. Then, together, you can find ways to support those dreams, or to adjust them. Use this exercise as an opportunity to figure out what triggers fear and why. In other words, tap into your fears. And instead of shutting your partner down, seek a compromise that feels good to you as a couple. In the case of Rich and Laurie, Rich wanted to be a really good dad but just didn't know how. He needed a little help. When Laurie was able to offer this help, the couple was able to continue growing together, instead of growing apart.

Change makes you grow, and only by sitting down together and talking about it can you make sure you grow in the same direction. Change comes in many guises. Maybe one of you wants to start working on improving your health. Maybe your pet passed away. Maybe the house has mold. Maybe you just turned forty, or maybe you woke up one day and said, "I don't want to do this anymore." For Rich and Laurie, and for many other couples I've worked with, change came from having a child. But you can do something about change with your partner. When change is in the offing, instead of being a spectator on the sidelines, get on the field *with* your partner. In this way, you can *grow together* instead of *growing apart*.

HEARTwork

Transforming Grow Apart into Grow Together

Exercise 1: The Grow Apart, Grow Together Quiz

Are you and your partner growing together or growing apart? To find out, read the following statements, and for each one, circle the number for the response that comes closest to how you feel.

---

1 = Strongly Disagree, 2 = Disagree, 3 = Agree, 4 = Strongly Agree

---

1. I wish I understood more why my partner loves the things he or she does.

                              1   2   3   4

2. I fear that if I keep growing, I'll grow out of the relationship.

                              1   2   3   4

3. It's hard to get my partner interested in some of the activities I enjoy.

                              1   2   3   4

4. We used to have things that we liked to do together. . . . I miss that time.

| 1 | 2 | 3 | 4 |

5. I have dreams and desires that my partner knows nothing about.

| 1 | 2 | 3 | 4 |

6. Even when we both have free time, we usually spend it doing our own things.

| 1 | 2 | 3 | 4 |

7. My partner's life plan is moving too fast or too slow for me.

| 1 | 2 | 3 | 4 |

8. I can't remember the last time we did something new that stimulated both of us.

| 1 | 2 | 3 | 4 |

9. Sometimes I look at my partner and barely recognize the man or woman I used to know.

| 1 | 2 | 3 | 4 |

10. When we're apart during the day, I don't really know what he or she is up to.

| 1 | 2 | 3 | 4 |

11. When my partner talks about his or her friends or the people at work, I have no idea who he or she is talking about.

| 1 | 2 | 3 | 4 |

12. Who has time for *quality time?*

| 1 | 2 | 3 | 4 |

13. My partner seems to value things that don't really interest me.

| 1 | 2 | 3 | 4 |

14. My partner and I don't talk as often as we used to; we seem to be leading separate lives.

    1   2   3   4

15. I'm trying to grow, but my partner seems stuck in the past.

    1   2   3   4

16. Now that we've made a commitment, I sometimes feel like there's been a bait and switch. It's not like it was when we were first dating.

    1   2   3   4

17. One of us is always trying to understand how the past affects the present, and the other has no interest in going there.

    1   2   3   4

18. One of us thinks the other is a stick-in-the-mud.

    1   2   3   4

19. There's too much water under the bridge, and we're just too different now.

    1   2   3   4

20. I don't know why I keep trying to explain things; he or she will never get it.

    1   2   3   4

21. My partner never tries to understand the parts of me that he or she doesn't get.

    1   2   3   4

Scoring: Add up the numbers you circled for your total score.

Below 35: It looks like you and your partner make an effort to face life changes, both big and small, as a united team. You each know what makes the other tick, and you look forward to the adventures you'll face together in the future. Spending quality time together is a priority in your relationship, and when you're feeling disconnected, you're not afraid to talk things out. If that sounds like you and your partner, feel free to continue on to the next chapter.

35–50: You and your partner used to share a circle of love, but lately you've been feeling that you're drifting apart—even when you're together. Start with the following HEARTwork exercises, and consider making some time to sit down and take stock of your relationship. Renewing your commitment to each other now may prevent the rift from widening.

51 or above: Things may have started out great, but now you often feel like you barely recognize the man or woman you used to love. You may already be leading separate, parallel lives. Closing the gap will require you to come together and get to know the man or woman that each of you has become. Start with the following HEARTwork exercises.

Exercise 2: Challenge Your Beliefs

Couples have difficulty navigating change when they hold on to expectations, standards, and beliefs long after they are no longer working or valid. Take a closer look at your views on the roles that the partners in a couple should assume. Make a list of the traits that you believe each partner should have and the duties and responsibilities they should assume. Do you believe your partner should be the primary or sole provider for your family, should initiate sex, or should do the cooking? Or do you believe that one person should be responsible for putting meals on the table, while the other should handle mowing the lawn? Maybe you believe that everything in a marriage should be fifty-fifty. Whatever your beliefs about the roles in a partnership are, record them.

My partner should be: _____

I should be: _____

My partner should do: _____

I should do: _____

Exercise 3: Redefine Your Roles

It's your job to figure out if your individual beliefs about your and your partner's roles are helping you grow together or forcing you to grow apart. Are you holding on to certain ideas about your roles just because you think that's what each of you *should* do? Are you willing to release some of these "shoulds" in favor of an understanding that feels more authentic? Are you willing to create new expectations? Are you willing to rethink stereotypes and your unsaid expectations in order to discover the comfortable and/or healthy roles in your relationship?

Look back over the list you made in the previous exercise and ask yourself where each of these beliefs came from. Was a particular belief modeled by your parents? Does it come from a general societal understanding of gender roles? Does it feel central to who you really are, or is this belief a "should" to which you conformed yourself? How many of the beliefs on your list actually originated with you? And how many do you really want to keep?

Think about the aspects of your relationship that do not conform to the expectations of society or your parents. Does your husband do the dishes? Does your wife make more money? If that works for you, great! That's what matters. Take the time to list at least three ways in which your relationship defies traditional gender stereotypes. If your relationship adheres to traditional gender prescriptions in all respects, list those prescriptions you wish you could do away with:

_____

_____

_____

Chapter 8

●●●●●●●

The Owner's Manual

THE OTHER DAY, I was in a long checkout line at the grocery store, and there were a couple of tables and chairs nearby. At one table was a couple in their early seventies. They were both sitting there and looking down at their iPhones, tapping away, pretty much oblivious to their partner sitting next to them. The whole time I was in line, they didn't look up for a moment. So it appears that twenty-year-olds and thirty-, forty-, fifty-, and sixty-year-olds are not the only ones who have forgotten what it's like to really be together. I wondered that day, if the couple put the iPhones away, what would they be saying? We broadcast all our most private details to people in the Twittersphere, but we forget to do the same with the person we sleep next to every night. If you're like so many other people out there who haven't had face-to-face intimacy with their partner for a long time, and you're curious but uncomfortable about trying to create it, here is your chance.

We've talked so much in this book about the opportunity to use what comes up in a relationship, that is, the conflicts and the fears that lie beneath, to heal these very personal traumas, big and small. The salve that cures all is your partner's understanding, completely free of judgment. To give your partner that experience really is the greatest gift that a human being can give to another human being. And it all begins with taking the time to be present with each other.

The HEARTwork exercises in the preceding chapters serve to help partners find their way back to each other. But there are also universal strategies that can help couples figure out how to start tackling the issues they may have uncovered in the HEARTwork exercises. This chapter is the most important tool in this book: it will become your and your partner's Owner's Manual. Your work in this chapter will enable you to get to know your partner in a way that no one else does, and it will empower you to create and strengthen an unbreakable bond.

For example, my husband, Eric, knows that I'm deathly allergic to poison oak, and he is always scouting for it when we go hiking. He even knows why I hate pickles and why I have dedicated so much time to rescue animals. And I know that Eric always prefers a home-cooked meal over going out to a fancy-schmancy restaurant, and on New Year's Day he has this ritual of always going surfing, so I know not to make plans. All these details add up to knowing your partner deeply and profoundly.

The conflict loops described in this book are often rooted in misunderstanding, the antidote to which is *understanding*. Why does your partner think the way he or she thinks and act the way he or she acts? If you truly know your partner, you'll know why. As we've seen with all these couples in all these chapters, understanding often comes by way of empathy, since empathy enables one partner to accept those aspects of the other partner that he or she may dislike, and thereby make a connection. The Owner's Manual fosters understanding, which creates more empathy, which paves the way for circles of love.

Here's the deal.

You might laugh, but some of you know squat about the person you love. This chapter offers you an opportunity to learn all about him or her by asking a series of questions. You can ask each other these questions casually as you cook dinner together, take a nighttime stroll with the dog, or enjoy a cup of coffee. Maybe you can even do some of the easy questions with your kids present so they get to hear about the fun stuff, such as how you met, what made you first love Daddy, what your favorite early date was, what your childhood nicknames were, and so on. Yes, some of these questions are really basic and might seem silly. For instance, do you really need to ask your partner about his or her favorite color? How can *that* save your relationship or help you grow closer together? The answer is . . . it helps *profoundly*. Some of these facts might seem like silly little details, but these details make up the person you love. Knowing these things about your partner—and letting your partner know these things about you—helps to form and solidify your bond. Such knowledge creates the feeling that he or she gets you like no one else in the world. Some questions may evoke more emotion for the one speaking or the one listening than either of you anticipated, so create a safe space for any more difficult conversations. Always check in with your partner first and respect a no or any boundary that he or she may have.

The feeling of knowing and being known can help you stay on the path to deep and abiding intimacy and love, and it can preempt conflict and disconnection. It's also the antidote to loneliness. Yes, you can absolutely be lonely inside a relationship—and chances are that if you're reading this book, you may have experienced this feeling. We assume that once we're in a relationship, we'll never be lonely again. Here's a reality check: it isn't true. There can be a great deal of shame in admitting you feel lonely, even with your partner, as if it's some kind of character defect. But loneliness grows not just from being alone physically, but also from being left alone emotionally. With its emphasis on knowledge, the Owner's Manual can help you and your partner come back together. It can enable you to find your way back to your partner and to the circle of love you once shared.

So begin to ask each other questions from this Owner's Manual. Ask a couple of quick questions each week to start discovering everything you need to know about the person you've decided to spend your life with. Then try to come up with your own questions. Muster up the courage to stand next to your partner and ask the tough questions. Maybe for the first time you'll learn that your confident wife used to be painfully shy (that's an evening's conversation right there). As you delve into such details in your conversations, you will come to know each other like no one else in the world.

GETTING STARTED: THE "EASY" STUFF

These questions cover the basics, and they have three purposes. First, while some of these questions seem silly, you'd be surprised at how many people don't know these basic things about their partners. For many couples, the basics aren't a trivial matter. For example, there may be a lot of tension every year about birthdays or anniversaries because one partner just can't seem to get it right. How many men do you see wandering around like deer in headlights in the lingerie department, looking for a gift for their wife? We often give our partners what *we* really want. Now is your chance to understand what your *partner* really wants. I love surprises, especially ones that let me know that Eric *gets* me. Gifts are just the start. Knowing seemingly trivial details can help you start to show your partner that you really get it.

Second, these basic questions can help you learn to have conversations again. If you aren't used to discussing deeper issues, such as feelings and fears, with your partner, you're going to need a bit of a warm-up to work your way into it. These basic questions will help you figure out *how* to talk to each other again.

And finally, like all the questions in this Owner's Manual, these basic questions are meant to be just the start— they're meant to prime the pump. For instance, if you ask your partner, "Hey, do you have a nickname?" you might actually learn much more than your partner's nickname.

You might find out that calling her by that nickname makes her feel all warm and mushy inside, or you might discover how painful it was when kids at school used that nickname, and so she never wants to hear it again. With this kind of knowledge, instead of thinking your partner's nuts because he or she reacts or behaves in a certain way, you might have an aha moment. Understanding can transform judgment into compassion.

These prompts will untie your tongue and start conversations. After you pose a particular question, try asking a follow-up why question to elicit a more nuanced response. But where you go from here is really up to you. Even the silliest question can lead to understanding your partner in ways you might never have imagined.

1. What is your favorite color?
2. What is your favorite flower?
3. What is your favorite food?
4. What is your least favorite food?
5. What kind of clothing are you most comfortable in? What kind of clothes do you hate to wear?
6. When you want to treat yourself, what do you do?
7. Which events do you attend and which activities do you take part in when you just want to play?
8. Can you tell me something I don't yet know about you?
9. Did you have a childhood nickname, and can I use it now?
10. What are some scents you love and some you hate? What memories are associated with these scents?

UNDERSTANDING WHERE YOU BOTH COME FROM

We aren't always conscious of the ways in which our childhood and our family experiences and our previous romantic relationships contribute to how we handle pressure, stress, conflict, and commitment. Take some time to explore your past and your partner's past. After posing each question, consider following up by asking "How did that make you feel?" or "Can you tell me more?" or "What was that like for you?" There is usually a story that goes with these memories.

1. Who was your best friend while you were growing up?
2. How did your family handle painful topics or events? Did they talk about them, or did your family sweep things under the rug and pretend that difficulties didn't exist or were no big deal? How does the way your family dealt with challenges affect you as an adult?
3. What was your role in the family? Were you the favorite child? The good girl or boy? The wild child? The black sheep? The mediator or "fixer"? Were you doted on or ignored? Teased or praised? Does this family role affect you now?
4. Who did you turn to when you needed nurturing? How successful were you at finding the nurturing you needed?
5. How was love expressed in the home? Was there a lot of hugging and kissing? Were you given lots of verbal praise?
6. How was anger expressed in the home? Was there a lot of screaming, yelling, or name-calling? Was there quiet tension? Was anger discouraged or ignored?
7. What happened when you accomplished something note-

worthy, such as straight As on a report card or scoring the winning goal for the team? Were you praised? Showered with attention? Given a gift? Were your accomplishments ignored? Were your parents not that impressed?

8. What happened when you got into trouble? What were punishments like in your family?

9. Did anyone in your family have problems with alcohol or substance abuse? What about overspending or gambling? Depression or suicide? Were these problems talked about? How were you expected to deal with family secrets?

10. What pressure did you feel from your parents? Was there pressure to do things, to act in certain ways, or to *be* different than you were naturally or you would have chosen to be?

SHOWING LOVE AND AFFECTION

We first learn how to express love by following the example our parents provide. Thus, someone who was raised in a home with lots of hugging and kissing may be very comfortable expressing love physically, whereas someone who was raised without much physical contact might not be very affectionate with his or her partner or spouse. Explore the ways in which your partner expresses and receives love and affection by asking these questions.

1. Can you give me a few examples of what I can do to make you feel loved? What makes you feel nurtured and cared for?

2. Can you tell me about one time in our relationship when you felt absolutely loved and understood?
3. What do I do that makes you shut down? How do I push you away? What would you rather I do?
4. What is your first memory of feeling loved?
5. Do you ever reject love or hold yourself back from loving?
6. What are three things (not people) that make you happy?
7. Was there a time when you felt happier than you thought you could ever feel?
8. Can you tell me about a time when I did something to make you feel loved and supported?
9. Can you tell me about a time when you needed me to protect you and I followed through?
10. What does *love* mean to you? Has your definition of *love* changed over the years or while we have been together? What does it mean to love someone and to be loved in return? How does it look? How does it feel?

UNDERSTANDING VALUES AND "BIG" EXPECTATIONS

Here's your chance to turn unspoken assumptions into mutually understood facts. You'd be surprised how many couples leave these big topics untouched. And you'd also be surprised how calming it feels to know you're on the same page—or at least to know where you've agreed to disagree. These are big topics, so consider giving each one the time it needs.

1. Did your family have any religious or spiritual beliefs, and how did your family's beliefs influence you as a child?

How do these beliefs influence you to this day? What values, or lack thereof, did or do your parents have, and did these values become models for what you did or did not want for yourself or your own family?

2. What were your expectations about how many children (if any) we would have? Has that changed while we have been together?

3. Do you like what you are doing for a living? What are your expectations and hopes for your career? How long do you see yourself doing what you are doing? Would you like to make a change in the career you have presently?

4. What kinds of commitments do you see us making with each of our families as a couple and individually? Are there any boundaries? In other words, are some of these commitments deal breakers or must-dos for you or them? What about holidays? And financial and emotional support?

5. What is your definition of *cheating*? What would be more devastating to you, an affair of the heart or a purely physical affair? Why?

6. How do you see us celebrating the holidays as a couple? Are some holidays more important to you than others? Is one holiday in particular the most special to you? How about anniversaries and birthdays?

7. When our parents become elderly and are in the final stages of life, what are your expectations about how we will care for them? Do you feel it is important to help financially? Would you want them to live with us or nearby so we could care for them?

8. How much "we" time would you like or do you think we

need to have a healthy relationship? How much "me" time would you like or do you think you need to take care of yourself and feel autonomous?

9. This may be hard to talk about, but what about when we become elderly? How do you envision us living the last chapter of our life? In a retirement home? Or will we stay in our own home to the very end?

10. Are there any companies, products, or stores you feel strongly about boycotting for moral, political, or humanitarian reasons? Why? And are there any companies, causes, or groups you would like us to support or volunteer for as a couple or a family?

EXPLORING REGRETS AND DIFFICULT MEMORIES

Respect your partner's boundaries. If your partner says that he or she is not ready to address the questions in this section, that's okay. If not, your partner may be comfortable with and open to exploring the fear that some of these questions provoke. That in itself can be even more valuable than the answer to a specific question. Pushing your partner to answer these questions or "do the work" could undermine your efforts to grow closer. Respecting this boundary can strengthen your bond even more than your knowing the answers. If you uncover something painful that needs to be healed, your next step is to ask, "What is an action I can take? What can I do to help you with that?"

1. Before we met, what was the worst date you ever went on?

2. What's the most painful experience that you have ever had?

3. Have you ever felt shamed by another person? Would you be willing to talk to me about it?

4. Is there any shame from the past that you still carry with you? Is there anything about yourself you feel ashamed of?

5. Can you tell me about one thing you did when you were young that you really wish you could have or would have done differently?

6. Has anyone ever been cruel to you? Where you bullied as a child or an adult? Would you be willing to share that with me? Do you think it affects you today?

7. Everyone has done things that are embarrassing, but can you tell me about a time when someone else embarrassed you?

8. When you look back at decisions and experiences in your past, what is one thing you regret? If you could go back in time, what, if anything, would you like to do over? Is there any advice you would give to your younger self?

9. Is there something you tried to change in the past and are still struggling with today?

10. Have you or has anyone in your family or in a past romantic or significant relationship struggled with an alcohol, substance, eating, or psychiatric (mental) disorder? How was it dealt with, if at all? How did it affect you? Do you think it affects you now?

ENVISIONING YOUR FUTURE TOGETHER

It's not only the things that have happened that make you who you are; it's also the things that you dream about for the future. Your hopes, your desires, the things you day-dream about are an important part of you, and your partner also has hopes and desires. You might not be used to discussing each other's dreams. But you might find that with some creativity, you can make some of these dreams come true. Maybe you can't build your partner a dream tree house with running water, but if you know that's a fantasy, next time you go on vacation, you might be able to rent one for a night. Now is the time to understand these hopes and dreams for your future together.

1. If you could take a fantasy vacation (forget about money), where would it be and why? Are you drawn to the ocean, the woods, a place that is deserted and quiet, or some-place bustling with people? Would you go with a group, or would it be just the two of us?

2. If you could live anywhere in the world and in any kind of home, where would it be and what would the home look like? Would it be a cabin somewhere deep in the woods? A villa in Italy? Would it be the very home we live in right now?

3. If money were no object, what would you do and why? Would you start a dream career or a charity? Volunteer at your local animal shelter or family services shelter? Maybe just play?

4. Where do you see us—and where would you *like* to be— in a year? In five years? Ten years? When we retire? How

do you see us loving our last act together, and how could we start working toward that now?

5. If you could change anything in our lives—for you, for me, or for us—what would it be?

6. If you were granted three wishes, what would they be and why?

7. If money, time, and experience were not barriers, how would you spend the next six months?

8. If you could change just one thing about who we are together as a couple, what would it be? If I could wave a magic wand and—poof!—our relationship would magically change, what would happen? How would that look or feel?

9. Do you see anything, such as a belief, a behavior, or something tangible, that limits your potential, my potential, or the relationship's potential? Do you have any ideas about how to remove or transform that limitation?

10. What could we do in the future to make our relationship stronger? If you could work on anything or do anything for "us," what would it be?

EXPRESSING GRATITUDE

Over time, the things you once loved about your partner—his levelheadedness when faced with stress, her spontaneity and sense of adventure—can become the very things that cause the most conflict. Dwell on the negative long enough, however, and you can get stuck in a negative rut. Cultivating gratitude is about more than showing your partner respect and appreciation. It entails retraining your brain so that you home in on the positive. Spend some time focusing on the positive aspects of your relationship, and you can reinvent the entire dynamic.

A good way to begin shifting your focus to the positive is by sharing memories that, as my father always used to say, "warm the cockles of the heart." It's amazing how revisiting happier times can open a couple up emotionally, and restart powerful feelings of generosity, empathy, and hopefulness. Plus, if you have children, this is a wonderful activity to do as a family, perhaps when you're riding together in a car or sitting down together at the dinner table. Don't underestimate how much kids love to hear stories about how their parents fell in love.

1. What was your first impression of me?
2. Do you remember all the particulars of our first date? Who asked whom? What did you wear? Did everything go you as planned?
3. What's your funniest memory from when we were dating?
4. When did you realize that you wanted to spend the rest of your life with me? Did you know all at once, or did you come to this realization gradually?
5. How do you remember my or your proposal or when we committed to each other?
6. What's your happiest memory from the previous five years? The previous year? The previous six months?
7. What do I do that makes you feel loved? What else can I do to make you feel that way?
8. When we first met, what was it about me that attracted you to me?

9. When times get tough in our relationship, are there memories that you hold on to?

10. What do you see as unique and even quirky (in a good way) about me?

TALKING ABOUT SEX AND DESIRE

It can seem like it's been *forever*. Maybe it has been a long time. For many couples I see, sex is the elephant in the room: it's not something they're comfortable talking about, but it's darn sure something they both think about more often than they'd care to admit. As with any habit, if you've gotten out of practice with sex, it can be difficult to restart. But, hey, it's also a habit that's like riding a bike, so once you find a way to come back together physically, it can be fairly easy to build it into the structure of your lives. Discussing likes and dislikes, as well as wants and needs, is a way to put sex back on the radar and makes many couples feel sexual, or at least that is a possibility! Use the following questions to begin a dialogue with your partner about sex and romance.

1. When was your first sexual experience, and with whom did you have it? Can you describe it? Was it good? Bad? Funny? Embarrassing? How did your first sexual experience make you feel about sex moving forward?

2. What do you think is sexiest thing about me, and what is the sexiest thing that I do, wear, and say?

3. Is there any part of your face or your body that you don't like or that you feel embarrassed about? (This is an op-

portunity to give that part of your partner's body a little extra love.)

4. What would make you feel more turned on? What's your favorite kind of foreplay? Your favorite position?

5. What are your turnoffs? (These could be little things, like bad morning breath or flossing your teeth in front of your partner, or these could be larger issues, such as aspects of your lovemaking, like needing more foreplay.) This is a time to be honest and open to honesty.

6. What are your sexual fantasies? Is there anything you would like to explore? Would you like to try one of them now or tonight or this weekend?

7. What was the best sex we have ever had?

8. Have you ever had a bad sexual experience that was humorous? What happened?

9. How has lovemaking changed for you as you've gotten older? Have your likes and dislikes changed in any way?

10. Do you have any sexual fears? (These might include emotional fears, like the fear that your partner might lose desire for you over time, or physical fears, like the fear that you'll become impotent, you'll gain weight, or you'll lose the body you had before the kids or when you met. This is a great opportunity to give your beloved a big, fat, healing reality check!)

3 Things You Can Do Today for an Instant Shift in Your Relationship

If you're feeling hopeless or ambivalent about your relationship, if you and your partner have grown so far apart that you're leading separate, parallel lives, or if you don't even know how to approach your partner to seek out his or her participation in revitalizing your relationship, focus on the following three steps. Little by little, you *will* begin to notice a shift in your relationship. When you're both feeling more open, you can return to and complete the Owner's Manual.

Give your spouse or partner a Daily Dose of Gratitude. Don't worry about beginning an official Gratitude Journal or coming up with at least three things that you are grateful for, that you admire, or that you appreciate. Find one nice thing to say to your spouse or partner face-to-face every day.

Ask your spouse or partner about his or her day. Don't unload all the highs and lows of *your* day first. Instead, focus on being a set of listening ears. When your spouse or partner comes home at the end of the day and has had a chance to change clothes, relax, and get settled, ask: "Did you have a nice day?" "How's that project at work going?" "Did you have that conversation with your boss?" "How was that phone call with my mother?"

Find time for physical affection. Everyone has different needs and desires, but we all have some degree of what I call "skin hunger," a desire to be touched physically. Find a way to express some physical love with your partner each and every day. This might translate into a kiss before work or a hug when he or she arrives home. If you've grown apart, take it slow. Even a gentle kiss on the forehead or holding her or his hand during a movie can restart the process of physical connection.

Afterword

· · · · · · · · · · · · · · · ·

CALL IT A magic circle or some good karma that goes along with this book, but at every step in the writing process, there has been an interesting coincidence: from the beginning stage in the creation of this book to the week it was finally submitted, people connected with the project fell in love or took their relationships to the next level. The week I was pitching this to editors, my wonderful agent got engaged. The editor who bought it was newly engaged and within weeks left to get married. The new editor who came on to replace her was engaged, and as I was writing this afterword, she was on her honeymoon, as was my agent! So call it a blessing, call it magic, or call it angels of love surrounding this book, but I really hope this circle of light surrounds you and your beloved, too.

The number one question people ask me over and over

is, "How do you do what you do? Year after year, how do you listen to couples' problems and pain?" My response is always the same. Yes, observing and listening to people's struggles can be daunting, but the joy and the privilege of taking part in the transformation of a couple's world from one of pain, anger, and heartbreak to one of commitment and love are so enlivening and far surpass the pain I witness. The process of transformation that I share with couples is the process I have shared with you in this book.

Regardless of our race, religion, sexual orientation, or political views, there is one universal desire, one longing that binds us together. This is the longing for a lasting, loving relationship. We want to look deeply into our partner's eyes and see that we are loved and accepted for our true selves. The rewards of a committed, loving, and ever-evolving relationship trump all the external, impermanent things that surround us. Homes, jobs, and finances may seem all-consuming and important, but they will never make you whole like a fulfilling relationship will, a relationship that provides a safe haven where together you can weather the inevitable storms we all face. These transitory crises become manageable when you have a life partner to hold your hand, to have your back, and sometimes even to be your guide.

Many times when new couples ask me if the passion they feel will stay the same, I say, "No, it will be different and richer and deeper in a way that comes only after creating a shared history. And in many ways, your passion will grow to be even more meaningful than what you are experiencing now!" But you can't merely stumble upon these emotional rewards or wish them into existence. Reaping these rewards in a relationship takes hard work and a commitment to examining the common sources of conflict you and your partner face and to growing together rather than growing apart.

Especially if you were raised in a home that had more conflict than love, realizing the emotional rewards of a fulfilling relationship takes courage and a commitment to finding new ways of being. If your childhood was tumultuous, you want something better for yourself and your family: a home filled with love, kindness, friendship, and laughter, a home in which pleasure outweighs the inevitable conflicts. As a child, you didn't get to choose your relationship with your parents. But the beauty of being an adult is that you get a second chance to achieve the emotional fulfillment that you may or may not have experienced growing up.

But the real reason I wrote this book is that we just give up too easily in our quest for a harmonious, fulfilling, and lasting relationship that grows stronger with time. If you've read this book, I know you have the desire, you have the intention, to create a long-lasting and fulfilling relationship. Just know there are going to be times when you take two steps forward and one back. It's going to be a rocky road, but it's one worth traveling. Remember, keep your eyes open for the good stuff, for the changes, and commit to appreciate each other and to address and work through conflict together.

This book represents an intention. Now you know how the negative interactional patterns you created in your past influence your present. But you don't have to take them into the future. You can make the decision to identify and break free from these patterns in the relationship and in the life you lead today. I truly believe that with a strong intention, the guidance in this book, and the inspiration of couples who have been where you are now, you can build a relationship that feels like the safest place in the world. I have seen some of the most solid, passionate, enduring, and enviable relationships between couples who got it wrong or struggled for years. No matter where you are in this process, taking the time to read this book, to take it to heart, and to test out the remedies and tools is a great first step toward a bright future.

I hope this book provides you with the hope, the tools, and the inspiration to believe that you are more than your negative behaviors and that you are stronger than these conflict loops. You are fully capable of nurturing and enjoying a relationship that lasts.

Namaste!

Acknowledgments

THIS BOOK ABOUT love and partnership was a labor of love involving all sorts of partners.

First, I owe a great debt to all the individuals and couples and families I have had the great privilege to work with. Their courage and willingness never failed to move me, and they taught me more than I can express.

I've had the good fortune to train with many skillful and talented teachers and mentors in the therapeutic community, some of whom have become close friends. Michael Solomon, PhD; Lewis Yablonsky, PhD; Ronald Alexander, PhD, LMFT; Louann Brizendine, MD; Virginia Satir; John Gottman, PhD; Stan Katz, PhD; Marion Solomon, PhD; and the Maple Counseling Center, where I did my clinical internship oh so many years ago, have all greatly inspired me. My colleagues in the Marin County chapter of the California Association of Marriage and Family Therapists have my deep respect and make me proud of our profession.

I have been profoundly influenced by the work of Salvador Munuchin, MD; Carl Whitaker, MD; Otto F. Kernberg, MD; and Heinz Kohut, MD.

I owe thanks in particular to Dr. Dean Edell, a friend and a role model, who showed me that media can be used to make the world a better place and who has long nudged me to "write a book." I offer thanks, too, to Ronn Owens, an always loyal friend and a superb talk radio host.

Jack Kornfield, PhD, and the great teachers of the Spirit Rock community have for two decades reminded me of the value of mindfulness, compassion, and gratitude. *Namaste!*

I am grateful to Eleanor Fields, my mother, who urged me to take the road less traveled.

My feisty and fantastic friends—Dr. Morgan Jensen, Bobbi Steger, Betsy Rosenberg, Dianne Fanning Flores, Vicky Livikas, Randi Braun, Sequoia Hoffstetter, Meli Cook, Debra Shelfo, Kathy Jacobson, Alyson Geller, Robin Zachary, Laura Marquez, Maritza Lizarraga, and Julie Shemano—always surround me in a circle of love.

Simone de Winter, Michelle Klink, Robin Gueth, and Rev. Karyl Huntley have kept me healthy in mind, body, and spirit; Katie McBride, a reference librarian at Mill Valley Library, has fed my voracious appetite for fiction; and Rhys Ludlow has taken care of business. Profound thanks are due to Rabbi Susan Lieder.

For eleven years Babette Perry, my beloved talent agent, who always has my back, has handled my media career with integrity and class.

Harley Jane Kozak, my best friend, a good mom, and a brilliant writer, has given me endless reality checks, occasional Tarot readings, and truckloads of lemons from her backyard tree.

And a big, fat thanks to the *Love Fix* team:

To my agent at Sterling Lord Literistic, Inc., Celeste Fine, for your expertise and inspiration and extraordinary instincts, and to Caitlin McDonald and John Maas, for all your support and helpful suggestions.

To Garth Sundem, who was there for the birth of the proposal and who rode in again like the cavalry at the eleventh hour to help with final revisions. Your talent was rivaled only by your enthusiasm, guidance, and skill.

To Cara Bedick at William Morrow, the Supreme Goddess of Editing, who is graceful, patient, and wise, who gets it and gets me. How'd I get so lucky? Thank you, Cara.

Finally, to my beloved Eric, for sixteen years of support and faith and the keeping of our circle of love . . . Words aren't enough. Especially these past few years, when I'd sit down at the computer for five minutes, which would turn into eight hours, when our "we" time got put on the back burner, and when life's other *mishegas* threatened to engulf me, your mantra of "You can do this" got me through it. My dear old dad was right: you are a man amongst men.

Resources

• • • • • • • • • • • • • • • •

The Gottman Institute study referenced in chapter 1 is discussed in John M. Gottman and Robert W. Levenson's paper "Marital Processes Predictive of Later Dissolution: Behavior, Physiology, and Health," published in the *Journal of Personality and Social Psychology* 63, no. 2 (1992): 221.

The study on how focusing on the positives in your relationship fundamentally alters the internal structure of your brain, referenced in chapter 2, is discussed in Alice M. Isen and Thomas E. Shalker's paper "The Effect of Feeling State on Evaluation of Positive, Neutral, and Negative Stimuli: When You 'Accentuate the Positive,' Do You 'Eliminate the Negative'?" published in *Social Psychology Quarterly* 45, no. 1 (1982): 58–63.

Gijsbert Stoet and colleagues' research on whether women are better at multitasking than men, referenced in chapter 3, is discussed in "Are Women Better Than Men at Multi-Tasking?" published in *BMC Psychology* 1 (2013): 18.

Arthur Aron and colleagues' research on the effect of learning a new activity with your partner, referenced in chapter 3, is discussed in "Couples' Shared Participation in Novel and Arousing Activities and Experienced Relationship Quality," published in the *Journal of Personality and Social Psychology* 78, no. 2 (2000): 273.

Richard A. Easterlin's study referenced in chapter 7 was discussed in his paper "Will Raising the Incomes of All Increase the Happiness of All?" published in the *Journal of Economic Behavior & Organization* 27, no. 1 (1995): 35–47.

Index

abandonment, 75, 92, 100–101
abusive relationships, 146, 161–62
accusations, 10, 48
acknowledgment, of your part in the
  pattern, 85–86
affairs, 154–65
  Caroline and Jake's case, 100
  ending all communication with
    "other" man or woman,
    158, 159, 172–73
  expressing anger about, 159,
    169–71, 173
  forgiveness after, 173–74
  healthy shame of cheater, 157–58,
    162, 172
  how to survive, 158–59,
    172–74
  Molly and Julian's case,
    154–64
  total transparency after, 159,
    164–65, 172–73

affection, 120–21, 252–53
  Owner's Manual questions to ask
    about, 242–43
alcoholism, 161–62
alliance testing, 190–94
anger, 129–31. *See also* Blame Game
    and Shame Spiral conflict
    loop
  ability to express after an affair,
    159, 169–71, 173
  Andy and Charlotte's case, 140–48
  managing body's response to,
    170–71
  processing, 148–54; for eggshell
    walkers, 148–51; for fire-
    breathers, 151–54
  releasing without dumping on
    partner, 169–70
anxiety, 27–28, 67–68
apologies (apologizing), and
  affairs, 154–55, 156–57, 159

"Are you in or are you out?", 15–16
Aron, Arthur, 81
asking, replacing testing with, 181–82
attraction, biology of, 24
authentic self, 107–11, 112–13

beliefs
    challenging your, 112–13, 232–33
    Francesca's case, 106–8, 110
    Owner's Manual questions to ask
        about, 243–45
    in Parent Trap conflict loop, 56, 71,
        72–73
    redefining roles, 233–34
    Susan and Tom's case, 211
betrayal, 99–100, 159–60
big emotions, 26–28
biological clock of women, 177
biology of attraction, 24
Blame Game and Shame Spiral
        conflict loop, 8, 129–74
    affairs, 154–65
    Andy and Charlotte's case,
        140–48
    Bob and Carol's case, 131–38
    fire-breather and eggshell walker,
        140–48
    HEARTwork exercises, 166–71;
        managing body's
        response to anger,
        170–71; quiz, 166–68;
        releasing anger, 169–70
    the in-laws, 131–38
    Molly and Julian's case, 154–65
    Sara and Sean's case, 3–4, 38–39,
        44–46, 48, 49–50
    3-Minute Fixes: heard and
        understood, 139–40;
        processing anger, 148–
        54; total transparency,
        164–65
Blame Game and the Shame Spiral
        Quiz, 166–68

blended families, 190–96
body, coming back to your, 40–42
boundaries
    setting, 56, 120, 134, 137, 145, 147,
        245
    testing, 181–82
brain, 24, 28, 43, 59, 64
breaking cycle of reactivity, 38–40
breaking the habit, 74–80
breathing, 38, 39–40, 170–71
budget setting, 78–79
"buttons," 20–22

Campbell, Joseph, 203
Celtic culture, 6
cheating. See affairs
"checking out," 10
childhood
    Andy and Charlotte's case,
        140–48
    exploring where you came from,
        113–14
    keeping family secrets, 161–63
    Owner's Manual questions to ask
        about, 241–42
childish vs. childlike, 57–63. See also
        Parent Trap conflict loop
children and parenting, 97, 222–29
    blended families, 190–96
chore play, 122–23
circles of love, 6–10. See also specific
        circles of love
Come Close, Go Away conflict loop, 8,
        12, 91–128
    four scenarios of, 92–94
    Francesca's case, 104–11
    HEARTwork exercises, 123–26;
        finding fulfillment in
        "me" time, 126–27;
        merging into "we" time,
        127–28; quiz, 123–26
    Jake and Caroline's case, 95–102,
        103

maintaining "me" in "we," 95–102, 103

Marco and Kara's case, 114–21

revealing authentic self, 107–11

Sara and Sean's case, 7–8

sex and the "When, Then" game, 114–21

3-Minute Fixes: being here now, 112; chore play, 122–23; natural self, 112–13; risk taking, 121; transition time, 103–4; where you come from, 113–14

Come Close, Go Away Quiz, 123–26

comfort zone, 189, 203–4, 220–21

commitment issues, Natalie and Owen's case, 176–80

common sources of conflict, 20–32

big emotions, 26–28

focusing on the negative, 28–29

great expectations, 23–26

life changes, 29–30

"When, Then" game, 30–31

"You're pushing my buttons!", 20–22

communication. *See also* Owner's Manual

ending with "other" man or woman of affair, 158, 159, 172–73

hearing with understanding, 139–40

complacency, 11, 13

compliments, 42–43, 64–65

conflict

common sources of. *See* common sources of conflict

four ways of diffusing. *See* diffusing conflict, four ways of

conflict loops, 6–10, 20, 237. *See also specific conflict loops*

control, 36–37, 54, 62, 74, 130, 142

cortisol, 27–28

courage. *See* emotional courage

Course in Miracles, A (Foundation for Inner Peace), 4

cultivating gratitude, 42–44, 64–65, 248–50

curiosity, 14, 35, 37, 70–71, 203–4

daily dose of gratitude, 42–44, 64–65, 252

deep breathing, 38, 39–40, 170–71

depression, 162, 208, 218

difficult memories, Owner's Manual questions for exploring, 245–46

diffusing conflict, four ways of, 35–44

breaking cycle of reactivity, 38–40

coming back to your body, 40–42

cultivating gratitude, 42–44

reframing conflict as opportunity, 36–37

distancer, 107, 113, 127

divorce, 3, 25, 75, 179

dumping, 159, 169

Dylan, Bob, 205–6

Easterlin, Richard A., 219–20

eating disorders, 161–62

eggshell walkers, 13, 140–48

processing anger, 148–51

emotional courage, 46–50, 69, 99, 122, 147

Marco and Kara's case, 117–18, 120

empathy, 95, 102, 237

enablers, 147

Equal Partnership circle of love, 8, 54, 56

HEARTwork exercises for transforming Parent Trap into, 82–89

exercises. *See* HEARTwork exercises; 3-Minute Fixes

expectations about relationship,
23–26, 66–71
Nikki and Shannon's case, 66–71
Owner's Manual questions to ask
about, 243–45
sharing of your, 73–74
exuberant child, 203–4

families, as source of conflict, 131–38,
190–94
family experiences
Andy and Charlotte's case,
140–48
exploring where you came from,
113–14
keeping family secrets, 161–63
Owner's Manual questions to ask
about, 241–42
family roles, 136, 190–91
fears, 10, 11, 13
challenging, 63–64
holding you hostage, 72–73
identifying, 63
fighting patterns, 4, 6–10. *See also*
conflict loops
fight-or-flight response, 27, 39
fights (fighting)
common sources of. *See* common
sources of conflict
four ways of diffusing. *See*
diffusing conflict, four
ways of
reactionary behaviors, 10–12
same fight, different night, 18–20
financial issues and money, 77–79
fire-breathers, 140–48
processing anger, 151–54
fixer-uppers, 55, 241
focusing on the negative, 28–29
foreplay, 115, 122, 251
forgiveness, after affair, 164, 173–74
futility, 7, 9–10

future together, Owner's Manual
questions to ask about,
247–48

gaslight (gaslighting), 68–69, 155–56
Gas Light (play), 155
gender differences, 59, 117, 177
gender roles
challenging your beliefs, 232–33
of Parent Trap, 59–61
redefining, 233–34
reversal, 214–15
Susan and Tom's case, 206–13
"get it all out," 129–30
goals
Owner's Manual questions to ask
about, 247–48
practicing mindfulness, 51–52
redefining, 215–21
Gottman Institute, 27
gratitude
cultivating, 42–44, 64–65,
248–50
Owner's Manual questions to ask
about, 248–50
Gratitude Journal, 65
great expectations about relationship,
23–26, 66–71
Owner's Manual questions to ask
about, 243–45
Grow Apart, Grow Together Quiz,
229–32
Grow Apart conflict loop, 8, 203–34
Alex and Hannah's case, 215–21
children and parenting, 222–29
designing new self, 206–13
HEARTwork exercises, 229–34;
challenging your beliefs,
232–33; quiz, 229–32;
redefining roles, 233–34
redefining goals and values, 215–21
Rich and Laurie's case, 222–29

Susan and Tom's case, 206–13
3-Minute Fixes: broadening
    your horizons, 214–15;
    considering what really
    matters, 221–22; role
    reversal, 214
Grow Together circle of love, 8, 203–4
    HEARTwork exercises
    transforming Grow Apart
    into, 229–34
guilt, 157

habits, breaking of, 74–80
healthy parenting, 58, 97
healthy shame, 157–58, 162, 172
HEARTwork exercises, 16, 236
    Blame Game and Shame Spiral
    into Ownership and
    Respect, 166–71;
    managing body's
    response to anger,
    170–71; quiz, 166–68;
    releasing anger, 169–70
    Come Close, Go Away into
    Interdependent
    Relationship, 123–26;
    finding fulfillment in
    "me" time, 126–27;
    merging into "we" time,
    127–28; quiz, 123–26
    Grow Apart into Grow Together,
    229–34; challenging your
    beliefs, 232–33; quiz,
    229–32; redefining roles,
    233–34
    Parent Trap into Equal
    Partnership, 82–89;
    acknowledging your part
    in the pattern, 85–86;
    quiz, 82–85; reframing
    "child" and "parent"
    roles, 86–89

Testing, Testing, 1, 2, 3 into
    Profound Trust, 196–201;
    loving behaviors, 200–
    201; quiz, 196–99; root
    of why you test, 199–200
hope, as secret ingredient for lasting
    relationship, 50–51
hopes and dreams for future together,
    Owner's Manual questions to
    ask about, 247–48
hostage, fears holding you, 72–73

infidelity. See affairs
inflexibility, 13
in-laws, as source of conflict, 131–38
intention, 40, 44–46, 50–51
Interdependent Relationship circle of
    love, 7–8, 91–92, 102
    HEARTwork exercises for
    transforming Come
    Close, Go Away into,
    123–26
intimacy, 94, 101, 120, 169, 235–36

job loss, 215–17

knee-jerk reactions, 3–4, 26–27
knitting circle, 208–9, 210, 213

Land of Me, 13–15
learning something new together, 81
life changes, as source of conflict, 29–30
listening
    asking spouse or partner about
    their day, 252
    hearing with understanding,
    139–40
    Sara and Sean's case, 1–3
loneliness, 3, 23, 123–24, 137, 238
love. See also sex and romance
    circles of, 6–10. See also specific
    circles of love

love (cont.)
    meaning of, 195–96
    mythologies of, 24
    Owner's Manual questions to ask
        about, 242–43
    loving behaviors, 200–201

make-or-break issues, 24–25
massages, 117, 120, 122
materialism, 221–22
meaning of love, 195–96
memories
    exploring where you came from,
        113–14
    keeping family secrets, 161–63
    Owner's Manual questions for
        exploring difficult,
        245–46
    where you come from, 113–14
"me" time vs. "we" time, 34–35,
    95–104
    finding fulfillment in "me" time,
        126–27
    Jake and Caroline's case, 95–102, 103
    merging into "we" time,
        127–28
mindfulness, 40–42, 51–52, 170–71
money and financial issues, 77–79
mothers, sleep deprivation of, 117
multitasking, 40, 59–60

nagging, 58, 59
natural self, 112–13
negative, focusing on the, 28–29
new self, designing a, 206–13
nicknames, 240

older husband and younger wife roles, 55
Ownership and Respect circle of love,
    8, 129–30
    HEARTwork exercises for
        transforming Blame

        Game and Shame Spiral
        into, 166–71
Owner's Manual, 235–53
    basic questions, 239–40
    envisioning your future together,
        247–48
    exploring regrets and difficult
        memories, 245–46
    expressing gratitude, 248–50
    fostering of understanding,
        237–39
    showing love and affection,
        242–43
    talking about sex and desire,
        250–51
    understanding values and "big"
        expectations, 243–45
    understanding where you come
        from, 241–42

parenting, 97, 222–29
    blended families, 190–96
Parent's Playbook, 228
Parent Trap conflict loop, 8, 53–89
    breaking the habit, 74–80
    childish vs. childlike, 57–63
    gender roles and, 59–60
    HEARTwork exercises, 82–89;
        acknowledging your part
        in the pattern, 85–86;
        quiz, 82–85; reframing
        "child" and "parent"
        roles, 86–89
    Nikki and Shannon's case, 66–71,
        79
    Phil and Leah's case, 74–80
    Susan and Stephen's case, 57–58,
        60–63, 66, 72
    3-Minute Fixes: challenging your
        fear, 63–64; daily dose of
        gratitude, 64–65; fears
        holding you hostage, 72–

73; learning something
new together, 81; sharing
expectations, 73–74
unspoken expectations, 66–71
Parent Trap Quiz, 82–85
partner's family, as source of conflict,
131–38
perfectionism, 57–58, 61, 225
physical affection, 120–21, 252–53
Owner's Manual questions to ask
about, 242–43
postponing. *See* "When, Then" game
premarital counseling, 25, 227
processing anger, 148–54
for eggshell walkers, 148–51
for fire-breathers, 151–54
Profound Trust circle of love, 8,
175–76
HEARTwork exercises for
transforming Testing
into, 196–201
pursuer, 107, 109, 113, 126

quality time, 31, 95–96, 232
quizzes
Blame Game and Shame Spiral,
166–68
Come Close, Go Away, 123–26
Grow Apart, Grow Together,
229–32
Parent Trap, 82–85
Testing, Testing, 1, 2, 3,
196–99

reactivity, 10–12, 13, 26–27, 48
breaking cycle of, 38–40
mindfulness for, 40–42, 51–52,
170–71
reframing "child" and "parent" roles,
86–89
reframing conflict as opportunity, 5,
36–37

regrets, Owner's Manual questions for
exploring, 245–46
risk taking, 121
role reversal, 214–15
romance. *See* sex and romance
routines, importance of, 218–19
rule book, 3
Rules, The (Fein and Schneider), 105

schedules, importance of, 218–19
Secret Ingredients for a Lasting
Relationship, 44–50, 120
emotional courage, 46–50
hope, 50–51
intention, 44–46
mindfulness, 51–52
self
authentic, 107–11, 112–13
designing new, 206–13
self-awareness, 20, 35, 39, 48
sensuality, 120–21, 252–53
setting boundaries, 56, 120, 134, 137,
145, 147, 245
sex and romance
in Come Close, Go Away conflict
loop, 93, 114–21
Owner's Manual questions to ask
about, 250–51
in Parent Trap conflict loop, 57–63
shame, 157–58, 160–63
Shame Spiral conflict loop. *See* Blame
Game and Shame Spiral
conflict loop
shared experiences, power of, 81
shouting, 13, 38–39, 141
shutting down, 13, 38, 48
Sisyphus, 76
sleep deprivation, of mothers, 117
sources of conflict, 20–32
big emotions, 26–28
focusing on the negative,
28–29

sources of conflict *(cont.)*
  great expectations, 23–26
  life changes, 29–30
  "When, Then" game, 30–31
  "You're pushing my buttons!",
    20–22
stepparents, 190–96
Stoet, Gijsbert, 59
stress, 27–28
substance abuse, 161–62
switching roles, 214–15
sympathetic nervous system, 27, 39

testing, replacing asking with,
    181–82
Testing, Testing, 1, 2, 3 conflict loop, 8,
    175–200
  Claire and Nathan's case, 190–94
  commitment issues, 176–80
  Dan and Cheryl's case, 182–88,
    189
  HEARTwork exercises, 196–201;
    loving behaviors, 200–
    201; quiz, 196–99; root
    of why you test, 199–200
  Natalie and Owen's case,
    176–80
  testing alliances, 190–94
  testing the waters, 182–88
  3-Minute Fixes: giving it a year,
    188–89; meaning of love,
    195–96; replacing testing
    with asking, 181–82
Testing, Testing, 1, 2, 3 Quiz,
    196–99
testing boundaries, 181–82
testing the waters, 182–88
  giving it a year, 188–89
3-Minute Fixes, 16
  being here now, 112
  broadening your horizons,
    214–15

challenging your fear, 63–64
chore play, 122–23
considering what really matters,
    221–22
daily dose of gratitude, 64–65, 252
fears holding you hostage,
    72–73
giving it a year, 188–89
heard and understood, 139–40
learning something new together,
    81
meaning of love, 195–96
mindfulness, 51–52
natural self, 112–13
processing anger, 148–54
replacing testing with asking,
    181–82
risk taking, 121
role reversal, 214–15
sharing expectations, 73–74
total transparency, 164–65
transition time, 103–4
where you come from,
    113–14
3 Secret Ingredients for a Lasting
    Relationship, 44–50, 120
  emotional courage, 46–50
  hope, 50–51
  intention, 44–46
  mindfulness, 51–52
time, managing "me" vs. "we," 34–35,
    95–104
time-outs, 38, 39–40
total transparency, 164–65
  as condition after affair, 159, 164,
    172–73
touch, 120–21, 252–53
toxic shame, 162–63
transition time, 103–4
trust. *See also* Profound Trust circle
    of love
  role after affairs, 154–64

tug-of-war, 91–93. *See also* Come
    Close, Go Away conflict loop

understanding, Owner's Manual for
    fostering, 237–39
unspoken expectations about
    relationship, 23–26,
    66–71

vacation from the Land of Me, 13–15
values
    Owner's Manual questions to ask
        about, 243–45
    redefining, 215–21
vulnerability, 13, 21

walking on eggshells, 13, 140–48
    processing anger, 148–51
walled off, 13
wedding rings, 6
"we" time vs. "me" time, 34–35,
    95–104
    finding fulfillment in "me" time,
        126–27
    Jake and Caroline's case, 95–102,
        103
    merging into "we" time, 127–28
"When, Then" game, 30–31, 116–17,
    118, 119, 218

"You're pushing my buttons!", 20–22

About the Author

∙∙∙∙∙∙∙∙∙∙∙∙∙∙∙∙∙∙∙∙∙∙∙∙∙∙∙∙∙

TARA FIELDS, PHD, LMFT, is a licensed psychotherapist who has been in private clinical practice for more than twenty-eight years. She integrates her passion for family systems therapy, mindfulness-based cognitive behavioral therapy, and self-psychology in her private practice, workshops, and media appearances.

She has been a keynote speaker, moderator, and workshop leader at Canyon Ranch (Tucson, Arizona), the Commonwealth Club of California (San Francisco), American Women in Radio and Television, the College of Marin, and many other organizations.

She has also been a frequent guest expert for numerous network media outlets and programs, such as CNN, *Dr. Phil, Oprah,* HLN's *Jane Velez-Mitchell,* HLN's *Prime News, Braxton Family Values, Hoarders,* and WE tv's *Fix My Family.*

Tara is a vegan and a passionate animal rescue advocate. She lives with her husband and her latest rescues in Marin County, California, where she spends as much time as possible outdoors, enjoying hiking, biking, and tree hugging in the beautiful San Francisco Bay Area.